BLACK FLAG DOWN

BLACK
FLAG
DOWN

COUNTER-EXTREMISM, DEFEATING ISIS
AND WINNING THE BATTLE OF IDEAS

LIAM BYRNE

Biteback Publishing

First published in Great Britain in 2016 by
Biteback Publishing Ltd
Westminster Tower
3 Albert Embankment
London SE1 7SP
Copyright © Liam Byrne 2016

ISBN 978-1-78590-095-2

10 9 8 7 6 5 4 3 2 1

A CIP catalogue record for this book is available from the British Library.

Set in Albertina by Adrian McLaughlin

Printed and bound in Great Britain by
CPI Group (UK) Ltd, Croydon CR0 4YY

CONTENTS

ABOUT THE AUTHOR

Rt Hon. Liam Byrne MP is a writer, reformer and campaigner. A former Cabinet minister, he did some of the toughest jobs in government in the Home Office, 10 Downing Street and Her Majesty's Treasury, where he was Chief Secretary. Before entering politics, Liam was a Fulbright Scholar at the Harvard Business School and a technology entrepreneur. He gave up a successful business career in 2004 to serve one of the poorest communities in Britain, his constituency of Hodge Hill in East Birmingham, where five generations of his family lived and worked. He has doubled his majority at every election.

Liam is the author of *Dragons: Ten Entrepreneurs Who Built Britain* (Head of Zeus, 2016), *Robbins Rebooted* (SMF, 2014), the critically acclaimed *Turning to Face the East* (Guardian Books, 2013), *Reinventing Government Again* (SMF, 2004) and *Local Government Transformed* (Baseline, 1996). He guest lectures at Oxford University.

ACKNOWLEDGEMENTS

This short book brings together years of research in my own constituency and across the Middle East. There are scores of peoples who have helped but who, because of the positions they hold, I cannot name. My debt to them, however, is immense.

I am glad to pay tribute to many others who have helped me so much – in particular, Chris Doyle, Chief Executive of CAABU (Council for Arab–British Understanding), which hosted my visits to Qatar and the Palestinian Authority (along with Medical Aid to Palestine); Gary Kent, director of the All Party Group on Kurdistan; and the Kurdistan Regional Government, which hosted me in Iraq. Prof. Linda Colley

(Princeton University); Dr Karen Armstrong; Dr Shahid Maher at King's College; HMA Vincent Fean; HMA Ajay Sharma; officials at the Muslim Council of Britain (MCB); Sir Trevor Chinn; Harvey Redgrave; Louise Casey; Ed Hussain, and the UK Embassy team in Qatar were all kind enough to discuss ideas and questions as they have taken shape over the years. Prof. James Arthur at Birmingham University has been a long-standing influence. In particular, I'd like to thank Chris Doyle, Nick Lowles at Hope Not Hate, Jamie Bartlett at Demos, and Talha Ahmad from the MCB for joining colleagues at the House of Commons for an extended discussion of narratives. I would especially like to thank Stephen Timms MP, Stephen Doughty MP, and my neighbour, Shabana Mahmood MP, for the discussions we've had. I want to thank Rt Hon. Stephen Timms and Gary Kent for detailed comments on the manuscript.

Most of all, though, the ideas here have been shaped by the constituents I serve and work with in Birmingham, in particular the leaders, parents

ACKNOWLEDGEMENTS

and students at Waverley School, Saltley School, Rockwood Academy, Washwood Heath Academy, Hodge Hill Girls School, Hodge Hill Academy and International School. Profound thanks go to Cllr Ansar Ali Khan; Aftab Chugtai MBE; Dr Iqtidar Karamat Cheema, Director, Institute for Leadership and Community Development; and the participants in our Hodge Hill Faith Leaders Roundtable along with Jonnie Turpie and the team at Maverick Television.

I'm hugely grateful to my fabulous agent, Georgina Capel, and Iain Dale for supporting the project, along with his team, Olivia Beattie and my superb editor Laurie De Decker. Finally, I owe a huge debt of gratitude to my parliamentary and constituency team: James Pignon, who prepared important research papers for this project, along with Gill Beddows and Sarish Jabeen. The errors are all my own.

CHAPTER 1

THE SURGE OF THE CENTURY

It was supposed to be 'mission accomplished'.

On Thursday 1 May 2003, a pink and sweaty President George W. Bush gently lowered his S-3B Viking fighter plane onto the vast deck of the USS *Abraham Lincoln* and, with the braggadocio of a cowboy, stepped out in his *Top Gun* fatigues to the salute of the flight-deck crew. A few hours later, he swapped the uniform of an airman for the uniform of a statesman, stepped up to a podium set before the smart ranks of marines, and boldly announced the end of combat operations in Iraq. 'The war on terror is not over,' he warned. 'We do not know the day of final victory, but *we have seen the turning of the tide*.' The giant banner behind him told a simpler, two-word story for the cameras: 'Mission Accomplished.'

Standing on the high mocca-brown ramparts bulldozed into the oil fields of Kirkuk, it didn't feel like 'Mission Accomplished' to me.

Here, on the 'Kirkuk field', oil has burned in the Eternal Fire known as Baba Gurgur since the Book of Daniel. Here, for millennia, shepherds have warmed their flocks on the plain's warm rocks, and the armies of the ancient east – Arabs and Assyrians, Greeks and Gutians, Christians and Kurds, Medes and Mongols, Hurrians, Parthians, Turkmen – have criss-crossed the giant flatness that stretches to the horizons. Here was the largest known oil field in the world until 1947, and here, today, the battlefront is still a continuous line of fire. The sun was beginning to set over the vast earthy-tan plain, burning the colour of the ground to copper. The hot air was thick with the smell of oil. On the horizon behind us, the great refineries were shooting burning gas into an ocean-blue sky. And through our binoculars, we could see, two miles in the distance, hanging limp on tall poles in the windless late afternoon, the black flags of the Islamic State.

In Kurdish, the word 'Peshmerga' means 'those who face death', and my guide, Commander Wasta Rasul, was a Peshmerga to his soul. His baggy sarsaparilla fatigues, topped with a natty Kurdish cummerbund, shrouded a prosthetic leg. His sagacious face, clipped moustache and easy manners projected a calm in command. Pointing to the bridge cut into the earth across a thin canal, he explained that here was where ISIS had tried to murder him a few months before with three Humvees packed with high explosives.

The Kurds have pushed the black flag fighters into a tight pocket between the oil fields and Baghdad, which lics 150 milcs south. But ISIS refuse to give up.

They fight on with a passionate intensity while the Kurds, dressed in a bewildering array of salvaged uniforms, armed with cheap but effective Russian machine guns and heavy mortars, often run short of ammunition. And the Kirkuk front is merely one frontline in a battlefront that stretches across a quarter of the globe.

Not long before my trip, a brilliant young intelligence analyst, I assume from the police, came to meet me in my Hodge Hill office, to talk through the sheer scale of the challenge to keep us safe. Over instant coffee with UHT milk and a few cheap biscuits from the Tesco behind my office, the officer explained the territory now open to our enemy that stretches across seven different theatres and several thousand miles.

'Of course we've got the caliphate but we've also got a lot more than that,' she said.

Al Qaeda is still out there and we ask ourselves what will they do next to get themselves back into the limelight? The younger element now might be more attracted to IS, but we've got individuals who have still got ties back to al Qaeda.

You've then got al Qaeda in the Arabian Peninsula (AQAP). They were behind the printer cartridge plot in the East Midlands. They're very capable and very capable bomb makers and they're constantly pushing propaganda at us through *Inspire* magazine. It is very practical with advice, for example, 'how to make an IED from stuff in your kitchen'.

Then you've got a al Qaeda in the Islamic Maghreb. Libya is now a vast weapon store. Al Shabaab is principally focused on the Somalian government, but they were behind the attack on the Kenyan shopping mall and they enjoy some support here. Then you've got Boko Haram, which is now aligned to IS. So what you can see is IS developing hubs right the way across the so-called caliphate.

This is the new reality: scattered theatres across an ancient map that together make up a battlefront of extraordinary breadth – dangerous, diverse, shifting and staffed with an extraordinary number of our compatriots.

Pressing on Europe's borders today is a tragic human wave of refugees unprecedented since the Second World War, organised by an army of people-smugglers. It's big business. Europol says some 30,000 people are now engaged in migrant-smuggling groups across the European Union, with 200 smuggling groups in Greece alone. Yet, as refugees beg to come in, the 'foreign fighters' are heading out.

The Combating Terrorism Center at West Point reckons that 'already in three years more foreigners have gone to fight in Syria than went to Afghanistan in the *entire* period of unrest between the Soviet invasion at the end of 1979 to the fall of the Taliban at the end of 2001'.[1] ISIS has perhaps 20,000 fighters under arms – an incredible five to ten times more

---

1   *The Group that Calls Itself a State: Understanding the Evolution and Challenges of the Islamic State*, issued by the Combating Terrorism Center at West Point, p. 82.

than al Qaeda. But worse: nearly one in five – 4,000 in all – hail from Western Europe. That's twice the number of three years ago. Seven hundred and fifty are thought to be British – an incredible 50 per cent more than in 2014.[2]

And what is extraordinary is just how easy it is to reach the frontline.

Three thousand miles from Iraq, I was sitting, this winter, in the Birmingham Crown Court. Court Room Eight is a big, scruffy room with a threadbare grey-blue carpet, fluorescent lights, long pine veneer desks with plastic water cups and, on the walls, lots of flat-screen TVs. Without the finely wigged barristers and the presiding majesty of a scarlet-robed judge, you'd be forgiven for thinking you were in a Travelodge in need of an update. In the dock, which is to say, behind some shatterproof glass screens, looking tired, pale and wan, was Tareena Shakil,

---

2 'Foreign Fighters in Syria and Iraq', Report to Parliamentary Assembly of the Council of Europe, January 2016, Doc 13937, paragraphs 9–12.

the 'student loan jihadi' and the first British woman to be convicted of IS membership.

As I arrived, the barristers were cross-examining a professor of Islamic theology on the whys and wherefores of *takfir*, the notion, of fundamental importance to ISIS, that a heretic could be lawfully murdered. In the banality of the Birmingham courtroom, the terms thrown around – 'the end of days', 'the Armies of the Mahdi', 'the Mujahideen of Sham', 'Hijrah', 'Shaheed' – sounded about as familiar as ancient Greek.

When the court clerks began to play the tapes of Ms Shakil's interviews, her sad story unfolded. With her slight Lancastrian lilt, the 26-year-old mum, who once loved *The Only Way is Essex* and dreamed of being a model, described the breakdown of her marriage not long after her little boy was born. It was clear she had suffered domestic abuse. Her husband drank too much and beat her. She dropped out of university and was gradually drawn to the Free Palestine movement. Soon, it seems, she was radicalised enough to hanker for a new life in the Islamic State.

Tareena claimed she was after a holiday – somewhere with plenty of Muslim culture, like Granada or Turkey. So she booked a flight to Turkey with some money from her student loan. She claimed she hated ISIS: 'These people are absolutely crazy. It's not from Islam what they do,' she said. 'Our prophet didn't drag bodies along behind cars … There are people in England who support them – but they haven't got the true information of what it's like. If I had the chance I would definitely speak to girls and say "it's not what you think".'

But the jury saw things differently. Tareena had posed for pictures with an AK-47. She had extolled ISIS's virtues on Twitter. She had let her fourteen-month-old toddler be photographed in an ISIS-branded balaclava. She was given six years in jail.

As the tapes played on the flat-screen TVs, I couldn't help but think of one simple thing: the journey from the mundanity of a Birmingham suburb to the monstrous battleground of Syria had taken as little as three days. Tareena Shakil had got on a budget flight from East Midlands Airport to Istanbul. She had met an ISIS recruiter – a very thin, skinny man with dark eyes and combed-back black hair she called Ahmed, on a hot, sunny beach in Anatolia. Within hours, she was in a cab with her suitcase and toddler in tow, and over the eastern Turkish border.

★ ★ ★

Yet, if the frontline was truly three days away, I think we'd count ourselves as lucky. But it isn't. Our enemies are determined to bring the fight to the streets of Europe, with tactics terrifying in their simplicity.

The battlecry went up on Monday 22 September 2014. ISIS's media-man, Mr Abu Muhammad al-Adnani, subsequently killed in the summer of 2016, issued a landmark call for attacks in the West: 'You can kill a disbelieving American or European,' he announced, 'especially the spiteful and filthy French … or any other disbeliever from the disbelievers waging war including the citizens of the countries that entered into a coalition against the Islamic State.' 'Kill him', he went on, 'in any manner or way.' In October 2014, Issue 4 of ISIS's magazine, *Dabiq*, hammered home the point: 'At this point of the crusade against the Islamic State, it is very important that attacks take place in every country that has entered into the alliance against the Islamic State, especially the US, UK, France, Australia and Germany.' '[W]e will conquer your Rome,' pledged al-Adnani, 'break your crosses, and enslave your women.' Al-Adnani repeated the call, just for good measure, in January and in March 2015, adding, 'Know that we want Paris by Allah's permission before Rome and before Spain, after we blacken your lives and destroy the White House, the Big Ben and the Eiffel Tower.'[3]

Ever since, ISIS's tactics have evolved from the

---

3   The 'Caliph' himself is a little more selective. Al-Baghdadi's five statements since July 2014 mention the West rarely and focus on the basic clash of civilisations: 'Indeed the Crusaders will be defeated,' he declared in November 2014, 'the Muslims will be victorious … the march of the mujahidin will continue until they reach Rome, by Allah's permission.'

ruthless hierarchy of the al Qaeda days to a perverse democracy of violence. Once upon a time, attackers – like the perpetrators of the 9/11 attacks – were trained abroad, tasked by top leaders and supported almost every step of the way. As al Qaeda came under pressure, links with leaders became looser, like the various al Qaeda plots by the Abu Doha network in the early 2000s.

As time went by, attackers began to rely on foreign experience simply for training. But soon terrorists were connected to handlers by links as thin as encrypted email, either with specific orders or simply encouragement to violence.[4] Now, we have the worst of all worlds. ISIS maintains the ability to plan and implement attacks from abroad – but just as dangerous is its ability to inspire 'lone wolf' attacks seemingly out of the blue. As one young counterterrorism specialist explained to me:

---

4   Like the Fort Hood shooter Nidal Malik Hasan, who exchanged emails with Anwar al-Awlaki without discussing operations.

With Syria, the threat has changed again. First, we had the declaration by al-Adnani, essentially inspiring people in Britain to take up arms – the 'lone wolf' attacks like the murder of Lee Rigby. [But] What the attacks in Paris and the Sinai and Lebanon and indeed Indonesia showed us is that IS now has an external planning capability too.

$$\star \quad \star \quad \star$$

So, the arc of the battlefront now stretches wider than ever. At home, our enemies' tactics are more dangerous than ever before. But what feels riskier still is the third revolution, the social media revolution that means extremists can knock up propaganda with the production quality of a pop video and move it at the speed of light on messaging apps from an iPad in Syria to the smartphone in the pocket of a youngster in the inner city.

Not long before I went to Iraq, I was in a classroom at Rockwood Academy in the heart of inner-city

Birmingham. Formerly known as Park View, it hit the headlines after I reported to Ofsted concerns from school teachers and teaching assistants that the curriculum was being undermined by some very unorthodox teaching. Within weeks, as I patiently tried to get to the bottom of what was going on with Ofsted, the Education Secretary, Michael Gove, put the school in the national headlines in what became known as the Trojan Horse plot.

Now, I was listening to a wise counter-terrorism sergeant talking me through the threat that worried him most. 'WhatsApp is a disaster for the police,' confided the officer. 'We think 80 to 90 per cent of our problem is the online world.'

The ISIS threat is peculiarly dangerous because of its toxic creation of a 'click and defect' model. The frontline is now online; not in the backrooms of mosques, but the chatrooms of jihadi online forums, and the journey from brainwashing to the battle-front is unbelievably short. Andrew Parker, the head of MI5, told Radio Four in September 2015 that 'MI5 has seen individuals radicalised to the point of violence within weeks'.

Key to the mix is the most sophisticated propaganda operation we have ever confronted, as one intelligence expert described to me:

There's a real sophistication in their [ISIS's] propaganda. It is very sophisticated. It appeals to disaffected teenagers with messages like the Knights of Lone Jihad. Worse, *Dabiq* magazine is now sharpening its focus on women with messages like, for example, 'To our sisters'. It is very different to al Qaeda. Once upon a time, it was all about supporting your fella. Now it's a direct appeal to come and help build the caliphate.

So in the propaganda you see a shift from beheading to focus on welfare services. And this we think has got a much stronger appeal to women. It works. This is an issue because the services are now dealing with people who are not known to us. Take the two girls who left from Bristol to go off to Syria. They had never even travelled across the city before.

Then, there's a threat from people who operate from abroad but then project back, like Junaid Hussain. Or others, who physically sneak back. What we worry about is their ability to mix with people who have been convicted of terrorism offences in the past but may now have served their time and be free back out in the community. And of course in many of these families there will be children.

Mission accomplished?

Every so often, the country's most senior counter-terrorism officer comes to spend an evening in Parliament and give a little situation report to MPs and peers.

And so, in one of the big committee rooms, red in hue with its gorgeous Pugin-style wallpaper, I joined some of my colleagues to listen in. In the corner, the caterers had laid out a few decent bottles of red wine and some nibbles. The sheer contrast between the civility of some chitchat over the claret and the horror of the challenge could not have been starker.

The bottom line is this: the advent of ISIS has been a game changer. We are now facing the surge of the century in terrorist activity.

As recently as 2014, al Qaeda and its affiliates were the most direct and immediate threat. But by 2014, ISIS took the lead. Today's wave of violence far outstrips al Qaeda. Al Qaeda tried to inspire individual operations by unaffiliated sympathisers in the West in the early 2010s, but its success was limited. ISIS has been *far* more successful. In fact, ISIS has inspired, on average, two sympathiser attacks every month since al-Adnani's call for individual jihad.

According to Andrew Parker, the head of MI5, 'the UK is facing an unprecedented level of threat, with Syria and Iran increasingly at the forefront of MI5's work.'[5] Some 60 per cent of counter-terror investigations are currently relating to Syria.

---

5   Andrew Parker, Radio 4 interview, September 2015.

As I write, not long after the fifteenth anniversary of 9/11, we have reason to feel we are making progress in the war against ISIS. ISIS has lost 40 per cent of its territory in Iraq, 5 per cent of its land in Syria and some 45,000 of its soldiers.[6] ISIS's Minister of War and propaganda chief have been slain. At home, hate preacher Anjem Choudary is behind bars. Yet this year has felt like a bloodbath. Some thirty-one ISIS-linked terrorist attacks around the world have killed 1,300 people and injured nearly 3,000 in France, Belgium, Germany, the US, Turkey, Libya, Egypt, Malaysia, Indonesia, Saudi Arabia, Syria, Yemen, Bangaldesh, Iraq, Kazakhstan and Pakistan. In the Orlando nightclub shooting, the US suffered its worst terrorist death-toll since 9/11. Iraq has been hit by the worst car-bombs since 2007. We're on the receiving end of the terror surge of the century:

---

6   See 'Former Commanders Take Increasingly Dim View of War on ISIS', *Time Magazine*, 31 August 2016.

- In 2014/2015 there were more terrorism-related arrests than in any year since the turn of the century.
- A fifth of all terrorism arrests this century have occurred in the past two years – 300 in the past year alone.
- We have now seen the youngest-ever convicted terrorist – a fifteen-year-old boy – sentenced to life imprisonment for inciting the Anzac day attacks in Australia.
- In June 2015, a seventeen-year-old from West Yorkshire became the youngest-ever suicide bomber, while referrals to the government's de-radicalisation programme[7] tripled.
- In November 2014, the Home Secretary said that since 7/7 the security services have foiled forty terror attacks – seven of which were in the past year.
- The murder of Lee Rigby in March 2013 brought the first fatality in the UK as a result of Islamist

---

7   *Daily Mirror*, Saturday 29 August 2015.

terrorism since the 7/7 bombings and, in November 2013, the head of MI5 told the House of Commons' Intelligence & Security Committee that there are now 'several thousand individuals in this country who I would describe as supporting violent extremism or engaged in it in some way that we are aware of'.

Mission accomplished?

That's not what the frontline thinks. Young mums can get on a budget flight bound for a Turkish beach and, with one cab ride, rock up in a war zone. Online, teenagers can be radicalised in weeks. Abroad, the theatres of struggle now stretch thousands of miles, from rural Nigeria to the borderlands of Pakistan, to nightclubs in Indonesia, while here at home, more of our fellow citizens are drawn into violence than ever before in our history. Thirteen years on from George Bush's descent to the deck of the USS *Abraham Lincoln*, we're not contemplating the joys of mission accomplished. We're confronting a revolution in the accessibility of violence. And we're fighting back in the wrong way.

THE WORLD'S FIRST GLOBAL INSURGENCY

It is, generally speaking, a good policy to know your enemy. And to know the kind of conflict they want.

When the Soviet Union fell, some said we had reached the 'end of history';[8] it was, said writer Francis Fukuyama, a glorious moment of triumph for democratic, Western, liberal values. In fact, it was without doubt a moment of hubris. Some, like the French foreign minister Hubert Védrine, were moved to label the United States the world's first hyper-power.

How different the world looks today. Together, ISIS and their allies have set out with breathtaking ambition to build an empire of intolerance,

---

8 Francis Fukuyama, *The End of History* (Free Press, 1992).

a 21st-century theocracy with seventh-century values that stretches from Portugal to Pakistan. It is a threat unprecedented since the Cold War. It will be defeated. The only question is how long it will take – and how much it will cost.

Many thirst for a strategy as clear and decisive as the strategy that defeated the Soviet Union. Back in 1947, the American foreign policy thinker George Kennan drafted what was known as the 'containment' strategy, later enshrined in Presidential Order NSC-68, signed in 1950. Kennan called for 'a long-term, patient but firm and vigilant' approach. But as the attack on the Twin Towers made clear, that is not an option open to us today. We cannot 'contain' our enemies as we did with the Soviet Union. We cannot allow our enemies safe harbour or sanctuary.

This is a very 21st-century conflict. ISIS may have imperial ambitions, but it is in essence an insurgency – an insurgency of intolerance – a form of warfare that is neither new nor narrow. It dates back to 164 BCE when insurgent Jews under Judas Maccabeus defeated their Greek occupiers and liberated Jerusalem, and today, it is remarkably common. The Rand group estimates that eighty-two of the world's 193 UN Member States are beset by some form of active or latent insurgency, thirty-five of which are beset by insurgencies inspired by militant Islamism.

Today, the CIA defines insurgency as quite different from terrorism, which is why ISIS is so much more dangerous than al Qaeda before them. 'The common denominator', says the CIA definition, 'is [a] desire to control a particular area. This objective differentiates insurgent groups from purely terrorist organizations, whose objectives do not include the creation of an alternative government capable of controlling a given area or country.' The British Army agrees: it defines insurgency as 'actions of a minority group within a state who are intent on forcing political change by means of a mixture of subversion, propaganda and military pressure, aiming to persuade or intimidate the broad mass of people to accept such a change'.

Down the ages, there are principles we've learned about beating insurgencies. Strategically, there is only one broad approach that works. Sun Tzu put it rather well several centuries ago: 'If an enemy has alliances,' he wrote, 'the problem is grave and the enemy's position strong; if he has no alliances the problem is minor and the enemy's position weak.' This was the idea that David Petraeus developed in the seminal 2006 US Army doctrine *Counter-Insurgency*,[9] which formed the basis of the Americans' surge in Afghanistan and Iraq: 'It is easier to separate an insurgency from its resources and let it die', wrote Petraeus, 'than to kill every insurgent.'

There you have it. We cannot kill our way to victory. To defeat our enemy, we must first isolate our enemy; cut it off from the wellsprings of ideology, oil, arms and the online world. That means cutting off ISIS and its allies from the support of foreign

---

9   FM 3-24 (MCWP 3-33.5), Army Field Manual 3-24: Counter-insurgency (15 Dec 2006).

states; it means cutting off its economy; it means cutting off its arms; but in the long run, most crucial of all, it means cutting it off from its ideas and draining the disaffection from where it recruits its troops, not simply in the Middle East, but worldwide.

We have to understand our adversary, which has to operate in secrecy – so intelligence is mission critical. Border control is vital in preventing cross-border infiltration and arms shipments. But the cardinal principle is this: military power alone is incapable of securing the defeat of an insurgency. Success or failure will always be decided in the political sphere. 'Political power is the central issue in insurgencies and counter-insurgencies,' added Petraeus. 'Each side aims to get the people to accept its governance or authority as legitimate.'

In the long run, there will be no substitute for building state capacity and, in the famous formulation of British counter-insurgency campaigners in Malaya, new governments must demonstrate the capacity to earn the public's allegiance by 'winning hearts and minds'.[10] So how are we doing at building a united front against our common foe? Faced with such an enemy, how would you fight back? Circle the wagons? Rally together? Forge a united front? Of course. Yet this is precisely what we are failing to do.

A DIVIDED HOUSE CANNOT STAND

Sitting in my Hodge Hill HQ, one of my oldest friends in Birmingham was explaining to the former Prime Minister's adviser on integration just where we're going wrong in the fight against extremism. Aftab is a local shopkeeper, chairs the local traders association,

---

10　Down the years, the use of combat force to 'search and destroy' has always offered an insurgent the best tactic for recruitment. It was Frank Kitson, a British army officer who led counter-insurgency campaigns in Kenya, Malaya, Oman and Northern Ireland, who observed, 'Firm reaction in the face of provocation may be twisted by clever propaganda in such a way that soldiers find the civilian population regarding their strength as brutality, and their direct and honest efforts at helping to restore order as the ridiculous blunderings of a herd of elephants.'

helps run some local schools and has worked on community safety for years. This year, one of his proudest moments was to visit the Palace with his mum and dad to receive his MBE.

The adviser had come to Birmingham to listen to a few home truths. And so I offered to pull some people together to tell it like it is. Aftab began by describing a conversation with a friend of his, who, like many people in Birmingham, came from Pakistan, like my grandparents from Ireland, in search of a better life in the headquarters of the Empire.

'My friend was telling me,' said Aftab, '"well, thank heavens; I never sold all my land in Pakistan. The way things are going for Muslims in this country, I don't know any more how much longer I'll be welcome here. You never know, do you, when you might have to leave and go back home".' The gentleman in question had served the Crown as a police officer in this country for nearly thirty years.

Far from forging a united front, our conduct in the fight against extremism has left hundreds of thousands of people feeling little better than the 'enemy within'.

Our enemies' weapon is not simply savagery, but suspicion. They want to divide and rule. Their numbers are small. They can never kill us all. But if they can turn neighbour on neighbour, then they would truly be in business. And the reality is, our enemies are making progress.

Now, it could be worse. We are not American – or French. We don't yet have megalomaniacs like Donald Trump trumpeting anti-Muslim hate speech. Nor are we blessed with leaders like Robert Ménard, the Front National's mayor of Béziers in southern France, the biggest town under the party's control. Mr Ménard was caught on film telling a family of Syrian refugees 'you're not welcome'.[11] But his party soared to seize 28 per cent of the vote in the first-round polls for thirteen French regions in December 2015, at a time when the authorities

---

11 *The Times*, 12 December 2015.

had to ban demonstrations in the Corsican capital after crowds began chanting 'Arabs out' during anti-Muslim riots. Just in case you were in any doubt about where they stood, the National Front's leader Ms Marine Le Pen declared, 'The war against France is being waged by Islamist fundamentalists bottle-fed by a lax sectarian Socialist party.'

So, it could be worse. But it would be wrong to get complacent.

Every few years, the British Social Attitude Survey asks people to self-report racial prejudice. The trend that has emerged over the past thirty years isn't great.

Between 1983 and 1987, over a third of the population identified themselves as 'prejudiced' towards other races. This fell to a little over a quarter in the years 1996–2001. But since the turn of the century, the figure has been on the rise. Today, nearly a third (31 per cent) of people self-declare as racially prejudiced. So: we are more tolerant to people of other races than in the mid-1980s – but less tolerant than at the end of the 1990s.[12] It confirms a picture that British Future found in their poll, which discovered 54 per cent of people thought that community relations had grown worse over the past ten years since the 7/7 bombings.

The situation is most acute for the 5 per cent of our neighbours who happen to be Muslim. In 2013, the British Social Attitudes Survey found that 62 per cent agreed that Britain would lose its identity if more Muslims came to live here – much more than the 48 per cent who agreed with the statement in 2003. Two years later, YouGov found that 55 per cent of voters in Britain thought that there was a fundamental clash between Islamic values and the values of British society, compared to 22 per cent who said Islamic and British values are generally compatible.

But worse is the surge in Islamophobic crime,

---

12 Source: 30 years of British Social Attitude Survey Self-reported Racial Prejudice data.

which has surged again since the vote to leave the European Union:

- In 2013/14, there were 2,273 religiously aggravated hate crimes recorded by police in England and Wales – an increase of 45 per cent on the year before. Nearly half of the offences were public order offences, principally causing fear, alarm and distress.
- In September 2015, the Metropolitan police released statistics showing anti-Muslim hate crime in Britain had risen 70 per cent in the past year. The Tell Mama project found that more than half of Islamophobic attacks in Britain are committed against women.
- The charity ChildLine reports that Islamophobic bullying is now afflicting schools, while a study by Teesside University found that children as young as ten had been involved in hate crime attacks.[13]

---

13   *The Guardian*, 18 June 2015.

My constituency is among the most diverse in the country – and it's also home to the biggest Muslim community in Britain. My Muslim constituents are overwhelmingly of the view that Islamophobia is going through the roof. Here are the results of a web survey I ran with my Muslim constituents at the end of 2015:

- Some 96 per cent believed that Islamophobia is on the rise in Britain.
- A staggering 87 per cent said that they or someone they know had experienced Islamophobia.
- Reports of Islamophobic abuse included people being punched, shouted at for wearing a hijab, having glass bottles thrown at them, and suffering racist remarks made in public spaces such as NHS hospitals, in the street while walking children to school and even while serving on jury duty. Islamophobia on social media is felt to be widespread – and companies such as Facebook are seen as doing little in response.

Here's a short selection of quotations from the web survey:

HAVE YOU HAD EXPERIENCE OF ISLAMOPHOBIA?

'Yes. A friend was punched and spat on whilst being told to f*** off out of this country. Called names including terrorist and paki.'

– *Male, 27, Small Heath*

'Several occasions, working with people who have never interacted with Muslims they have a common perception of hatred towards all of them, generalised label of terrorist, mockery, offensive jokes, some people use even threatening behaviour, intimidation, you name it. Sad state of affairs to know that so many people can be so horrible simply because of a label and misunderstanding.'

– *Male, 33, Hodge Hill*

'Been called names and my friend was thrown glass bottles at because she is also a hijabi.'

– *Female, 34, B33*

'Yes I was sworn at and told to go back to my own country, which I said fine it's only down south in Wales.'
– *Female, 43, Ward End*

'Whilst serving on jury service my wife had other jury
members making racist remarks due to the fact she was
wearing a hijab.'
– *Male, 33, Ward End*

'Being a courier driver going into certain areas I don't
feel safe anymore. The way I'm stared at as if I don't belong here. Also a couple of my female family members
have had verbal abuse aimed at them on the bus going
into city centre etc.'
– *Male, 31, Washwood Heath*

'I have experienced it in every form you can imagine;
physical assaults, being spat at, being sworn at, having
alcohol thrown on me. I do not feel safe alone in non-
Muslim areas.'
– *Male, 24, Ward End*

'Yes, at work as it happens. Colleagues thought I had/
have associations or affiliation with ISIS! Seems that if

you are a Muslim then by default that makes you an extremist or dare I say terrorist. The ignorance is truly shocking and unbelievable, what's more disturbing is how the media want to sensationalise the smallest event or incident.'
– *Male, 44, Washwood Heath*

'Yes it is rife on social media and Facebook does NOTHING to stop it. Once reported its dismissed as not violating any terms and conditions.'
– *Female, 22, Ward End*

'There is plenty of Islamophobia on social media which is upsetting to read as it targets both my family and myself.'
– *Male, 40, Bordesley Green*

'While walking my kids to school. An English man shouted from his work van why you wearing that thing for, meaning my head scarf.'
– *Female, 41, Bordesley Green*

So: we face a revolution in the accessibility of violence. To win, we need to stand united and yet, thirteen years after the end of combat operations in Iraq, we feel more divided than before.

For these simple, basic, blunt reasons we need to rethink our strategy for defeating extremism. And that rethink needs to start with a simple insight into the battle we're fighting. Today, instead of isolating enemies, we alienate our friends, our neighbours and our fellow citizens who happen to be young, idealistic, perhaps angry and Muslim. Online, we are without a grand alliance to tackle extremists on the digital battlefront. And in the Middle East, we're failing to build the coalitions needed to isolate and overwhelm our enemies. The fundamental point is this: to win you need politics, and to win in politics, you need first to win the battle of ideas.

CHAPTER 2

THE CLASH OF CIVILISATIONS?

igh up in the towers of Scotland Yard is a long, hot,
cavernous room that is home to one of Britain's
most important teams fighting the good fight against
extremism. The Counter Terrorism Internet Referral
Unit (CTIRU) is an extraordinarily small collection
of young police officers tasked with monitoring and
taking down extremist content from the internet,
whenever and wherever it is found.

The desks are crammed in so that the room resem-
bles a call centre, overloaded with gigantic computer

screens, over which, hanging from the low ceiling and fluorescent light strips, are laminated signs with the flags and insignia of the extremist groups that are the operator's targets. Here, sealed off from any electronic spies and eavesdroppers, behind heavy signal-jamming doors, I sat down to hear about the sorts of extremist propaganda blocked from reaching our children every day.

The team represent British policing at its best: full of practical wisdom and good, old-fashioned common sense, blessed with bonhomie and determination, patriotic to the core. And just to get us going, they thought I might like to see a 'classic' ISIS recruitment video. Over the next three minutes, I watched, mesmerised.

To rapid, pulsing techno beats, a deep, authoritative English voice narrated an entrancing story to dizzying, fast-paced video cuts of war zones, bomb blasts, slim and uniformed fighters armed to the teeth and smiling cheerfully, shocking scenes of destruction, spliced through with graphics setting out the scale of ISIS's triumph against the world; the vast diversity of its armies; the incredible odds against which it has fought and won; snippets of the Quran, justifying its cause; and scenes of horrible deaths suffered by Muslim children in Palestine, in Iraq, in Syria. It was the video-cinematic equivalent of an adrenalin-fuelled ride on the Nemesis roller-coaster, with the production quality of *Call of Duty*.

Shot through the subtext were some very simple, compelling ideas. Muslims are under attack. We need to defend ourselves. The world is throwing everything at us – but still we're winning. God is on our side. And we will win. I was speechless. I had never seen anything like it in my life. I began to understand the sheer scale of the battle of ideas in which we're now engaged, as seventh-century theology is married to 21st-century cinematography.

ISIS is crystal-clear about the importance of the media battle. The current leader of al Qaeda, Ayman al-Zawahiri, once declared, 'More than half of this battle is taking place in the battlefield of the media.

We are in a media battle, in a race for the hearts and minds of our ummah.'[14]

There are now many studies of the 'jihadi ideology'[15] and its propaganda, but when you sit down and analyse it, it becomes pretty clear just why it is so powerful: it combines what I call the 'five Ps of extremism'.

First, there is a very simple appeal to **piety**. Like all heretics, ISIS and al Qaeda make a strong claim to speak as the 'true believers' of Islam, and crucially offer a religious justification for violence. As Dostoevsky explained with regard to the moral dilemmas of *Crime and Punishment*, killing people is hard. It's why so many violent extremists have a criminal past; they have already crossed a line.

---

14   Ayman al-Zawahiri, 2015, quoted in *The Group that Calls Itself a State*, Combating Terrorism Center, op. cit., p. 86.

15   See, for instance, Charlie Winter's work for Quilliam, 'Documenting the Virtual "Caliphate"'; Tony Blair Faith Foundation's 'Inside the Jihadi Mind', which researched ISIS, Jabhat al-Nusra Front and al Qaeda in the Arabian Peninsula (AQAP); and the work of the Combating Terrorism Center at West Point, ibid.

ISIS, therefore, goes to great lengths to try and stack up Quranic justifications for violence. One analysis found that justifications from the Quran, Hadith (stories from the life of Muhammad) or other scholarship appear in almost all of its propaganda,[16] with citations from up to forty-five different scholars and references to up to 114 different Quranic verses.[17] Doctrinally, all share a Salafi jihadist approach, characterised by a rejection of those with whom they disagree.

The second 'p' is a sense of **pride**. It's a simple message: 'There's nobility, and chivalry in service and sacrifice to the cause', and advocacy of the oppressed. ISIS and al Qaeda both make strong appeals to a conjured sense of honour in service and sacrifice, much in the same way that stories of King Arthur and the

---

16 87 per cent, to be precise.

17 Key to the ISIS theological argument is what's called the 'prophetic methodology': claiming to be the prophet's successors; the idea of *tawhid*, or the unity of god, in contrast to *shirk*, or polytheism; and the notion of *takfir*, which is that killing of 'apostates' is permissible.

Knights of the Round Table were once used to inspire young men to fight in the Crusades. The iconography stresses the 'nobility' of jihad, with references to Saladin, pictures of fighters on horseback, heroes and knights. Even children are referred to as 'lion cubs'. In some studies, this is the dominant theme. A typical AQAP eulogy might describe how 'he [the "martyr"] was devoted to performing the Quranic obligation of fighting evil in the world' along with many variations of 'we love death as you love life': a romantic appeal to the virtues of dying for a cause, and the notion of 'service to the ummah' – the community of Muslims bound together by their faith – which is closely tied to advocacy for the oppressed.

Third, is **potency**. Both ISIS and al Qaeda have absorbed the lesson of Osama bin Laden, who said in 2001, 'When people see a strong horse and a weak horse, by nature, they will like the strong horse.'[18]

---

18 *The Group That Calls Itself a State*, Combating Terrorism Center, op. cit., p. 86.

So both promote a 'winner's narrative' of ever-expanding borders. ISIS likes the idea that they are the underdogs who win against the odds, so it's especially important for them to be seen as constantly on the offensive.

Fourth is **perfection**. ISIS and al Qaeda offer a cause they argue is worth fighting for: a utopian place, the new caliphate in which the ideals of Muhammad's life are revived and brought to life once more. One survey found that about half of ISIS propaganda depicts happy civilian life, with lots of images of religious activity, a flourishing economic life, delivery of justice for religious crime and effective local governance, such as cleaning the streets, fixing pylons and running clinics or classrooms.

By far the most important 'P' is the sense of **provocation**, a powerful feeling of victimhood, offering graphic evidence of civilian casualties and framing the struggle with the West as a 'defensive jihad'. In this, the extremists seek to exploit the basic instinct of Islam: the desire for justice.

Many in the West fail to appreciate the fundamental significance of justice to Islam. Yet, as the theologian Karen Armstrong writes, 'Social justice is … *the* crucial virtue of Islam.'[19] The journey of the Arab businessman, Muhammad ibn Abdallah, who became the Prophet, began with his observations on the crisis in Arab society. His tribe, the Quraysh, had become rich traders. But their nomadic code, which proselytised a care for the less fortunate, was in jeopardy. In the religion that emerged, Muhammad stressed how it was wrong to build a private fortune but good to share wealth and care for the vulnerable. This is a teaching that is enshrined in a tradition of alms or *zakat* and Ramadan – a month-long reminder of the privations of the poor, unable to afford to eat or drink.

ISIS ruthlessly seeks to appeal to this sense of justice to inspire attacks on the West. A typical exhortation might run: 'It wasn't the Muslims who

---

19   Karen Armstrong, *Islam* (Phoenix, 2001), p. 5.

dragged civilians into this war. It was the Americans, and on a scale that is astronomically different than ours. They killed millions of Muslim civilians in cold blood during the embargo of Iraq which was before 9/11.'[20] The extremists present their struggle as a battle for the end of humiliation of the ummah; 'It is crystal clear,' runs one AQAP article, that 'all jihadi attacks on the West came as a belated reaction to the tremendous Western oppression of Muslims.'

Sometimes, in the West, we act as if we are surprised by the power of this new ideological challenge. We shouldn't be, for its roots are over a century old, and they stretch far back into the days of colonial rule and our carve-up of the Ottoman Empire.

If there was a defining moment, it was perhaps the day in 1924 when Turkey's new and avowedly secular leader Mustafa Kemal Atatürk abolished the caliphate, enshrined as the Ottoman Empire, which had stood since 1299. The First World War

---

20 *Inspire*, spring 2014.

in the Middle East had come to an early end in 1914, but immediately the old Ottoman Empire was torn apart by a new struggle between Atatürk's modernising politics and the old Sultan, now backed by the British.

At around 8 a.m. on Friday 17 November 1922, a car with the acting dragoman of the British embassy along with General Harrington's aide de camp drew up at a side entrance to the Sultan's palace in Constantinople. The moment the guard changed, the last Caliph, Mehmed VI, his son and six of the palace staff stole into the vehicle, which sped off to the British naval base, to transfer by barge to the battleship *Malaya*. On board, the Sultan was greeted in the name of the King by Admiral Sir Osmond de Beauvoir Brock before the ship immediately steamed off for Malta.[21] A year and a half later, on Monday 3 March 1924, a 23-clause bill was presented to the Turkish National Assembly, replete with Article 1

---

21 *Yorkshire Evening Post*, Friday 17 November 1922.

declaring 'The Caliph is deposed'. It was passed by acclamation.

In the years that followed, across the East, gurus inspired networks, networks shaped nations, and two nations in particular; the region's theological superpowers, Saudi Arabia and Iran, began the faith race that helps define the Middle East today.

'Islamism', as it is unhelpfully known, has many well-springs, but arguably, there are four founding fathers – two Egyptians, a Pakistani and an Iranian – all inspired in their own way by a reaction to the colonialism of the interwar years.

Hassan al-Banna (1906–1949) was the son of an imam and watchmaker, and began his career as a teacher in the Suez Canal Zone. Shocked at the secularism and materialism of Isma'iliyah, the town where he worked, al-Banna saw around him an embodiment of the evils besetting Egypt, dominated by foreign capital and culture. And so he founded the Muslim Brotherhood, inspired by labourers in a British camp who implored him to deliver them from foreign domination.

The 'Brothers' could see the West dividing up the Middle East and, in the aftermath of the caliphate's abolition, they devised a simple slogan: the Quran is our constitution. Islam, they argued, was a complete and total system with no need to resort to European values. 'No regime in this world', wrote al-Banna, 'will supply the renascent nation with what it requires in the way of institutions, principles, objectives, and sensibilities to the same extent that Islam supplies every one.'

The Brothers' goal was simple and ambitious: the creation of an Islamic State in which they would implement the law of the sacred texts, sharia, as the Caliphs had done. It was of course profoundly anti-democratic. Political parties were scorned because their quarrels disturbed the unity of the duty of the faithful. The creed was by definition anti-nationalist, and in the post-war political violence that wracked Egypt, al-Banna was assassinated and Nasser, the leader of the Nationalists, took power.

Around the time al-Banna created the Society

of Muslim Brothers in Egypt, Abul A'la Maududi (1903–1979) was publishing his first book, *Al Jihad fil-Islam* ('Jihad in Islam'), setting out a vast ambition: an Islamic State covering the whole of India, delivered by a somewhat Leninist model of 'Islamisation from above'. Trained as an ulama (religious scholar), Maududi became a journalist, and one of the most prolific Islamist writers of the twentieth century.

God alone, he argued, must be seen as the source of the law.[22] 'The struggle for retaining control over the organs of the state, when motivated by the urge to establish the *Dīn* (religion) and the Islamic sharia and to enforce the Islamic injunctions, is not only permissible but positively desirable and as such obligatory,'[23] he once wrote. All people must submit to this law, and the sole mandate of the Islamic state

---

22 This is the idea of *tawhid* as a theological and political ideal.

23 *Princeton Readings in Islamist Thought: Texts and Contexts from al-Banna to Bin Laden*, edited by Roxanne Euben and Muhammad Qasim Zaman (Princeton University Press, 2009), p. 12.

is to implement it. Like al-Banna, he saw Islam as a complete system of life – 'a practical, social, political and constitutional reality – a live force to fashion all facets of our life',[24] and he believed a state operating in the name of Allah and implementing sharia law was the only possible safeguard for India's endangered Muslims. Pakistan's founders rejected the idea. In Pakistan, they wanted a Muslim state, not an Islamic State. But Maududi's argument and his organisation, Jamaat-e-Islami, founded in 1941, were hugely influential. And one man, Sayyid Qutb (1906–66), 'the philosopher of Islamic terror',[25] seized on the notion that an Islamic State, secured by revolution, was the way to power.

Qutb's worldview was profoundly influenced by colonial Egypt in general, and the Society of Muslim Brotherhood in particular. Like others, he saw

---

24 Quoted in Euben and Zaman, ibid., p. 88.

25 See Paul Berman, 'The Philosopher of Islamic Terror', *New York Times*, http://www.nytimes.com/2003/03/23/magazine/the-philosopher-of-islamic-terror.html?pagewanted=all&_r=0

Islam as a complete way of life. 'The history of Islam,' he wrote, 'is the history of the true application of Islam – in people's conceptions and their practices, in their lives and their social systems. Islam is the fixed axis, around which people's lives revolve in a fixed frame.'[26] 'Islam', he wrote elsewhere, 'is intended to penetrate into the veins and arteries of the society and to form a concrete organised movement designed to transform it into a vibrant dynamic community.'[27]

Qutb came to describe the world of his time as a state of pagan ignorance, or *jahiliyya*: characterised by a pervasive moral bankruptcy triggered by man's attempt to usurp God's authority and create governments of their own. He condemned both Arab nationalists and socialists, and argued the solution was to restore Islamic law as the sole source of sovereignty: 'Both individualist and collective [states]

---

26 Euben and Zaman, op. cit., p. 15.

27 Euben and Zaman, ibid., p. 132.

have ended in failure; neither of these nor any others have this revivalist spirit. At this critical moment of confusion and disorder, the time of Islam and the ummah has arrived.'[28]

Qutb's books, *In the Shadow of the Quran* and *Signposts on the Road*, both written in the 1960s, became bestsellers all over the Islamic world, with vast consequences. Qutb argued that revolutionary force was needed – 'A vanguard resolved to stay the course and navigate the vast sea of Jahiliyya that has taken root in every region on earth'[29] – and that those living in *jahiliyya* were no longer Muslims. They were, in fact, *takfir*, and therefore excommunicated; when one is *takfir*, 'his blood is forfeit', and such people were condemned to death.

Yet, neither al-Banna or Maududi or Qutb had anything like the impact of the radical Iranian cleric Ayatollah Khomeini (1902–89). Khomeini had first set

---

28   Euben and Zaman, ibid., p. 137.
29   Euben and Zaman, ibid., p. 139.

out his ideas while in exile, in his book *Islamic Government*, published in 1971. It was the first time a leading Shi'ite cleric had thrown his full weight as a doctor of law behind the ideas of modern Islamist intellectuals, preaching the destruction of the established order.

Khomeini had a long history of opposition to the Shah of Iran, violently denouncing the Shah's alliance with America in the early 1960s, which prompted his deportation to the holy city of Qom, from where he wrote his lectures. In a radical break with the Shi'ite tradition of passive resistance, Khomeini now called for the overthrow of the monarchy and the establishment of an Islamic government guided by a doctor of Shi'ite law as the supreme guide. It was a potent argument for theocracy that duly swept Tehran in 1979.

At first, the 'force multiplier' for these important thinkers was a wealth of social networks that had taken shape during the days of Western colonial government. Networks such as the Deobandi, which were formed just north of Delhi after the Indian Mutiny of 1857, provided a corpus of precise rules that sought to help Muslims live in a non-Islamic society without coming to harm, but which stretched across the Islamic world, collecting donations, organising trade, connecting people for work, arranging marriages and sharing subsidies.

At first, the new nationalist Arab governments created after the Second World War kept religion marginal to national life. They divided their loyalties between the Soviet Union[30] and the United States.[31] But, over the course of the 1960s and 1970s, 'political Islam' made the leap from social networks to states, as a 'faith race' between Saudi Arabia and Iran took shape.

During the 1960s, many of the Muslim Brotherhood were exiled to Saudi Arabia, where they helped to found the University of Madinah in 1961 and, a year

---

30 The USSR's allies included Egypt, the Syrian and Iraqi Ba'athists, Gaddafi's Libya, Algeria, southern Yemen and Indonesia.

31 America's regional allies included Turkey, Tunisia and Saudi Arabia.

later, the Muslim World League, which became the first coherent institution to begin shipping Wahhabi Islam worldwide. When the global oil shock transformed Saudi wealth, there was suddenly a fortune to spend on opening Muslim World League offices in every corner of the world, to spread Islamic Associations far and wide, to build some 1,500 mosques, and of course to print Wahhabi texts.[32]

But with the Ayatollah's surge to power in Iran in 1979, the 'faith race' took on new dimensions. Throughout the 1980s, as communism collapsed and nationalism lost its lustre, Saudi Arabia and Iran sought to extend their influence. While Iran backed the creation of Hezbollah in Lebanon, the Saudis sought a win–win deal with the Americans to oppose the Soviet Union in Afghanistan. While Hezbollah were pioneering suicide attacks, in the camps and training grounds of Pakistan's North-West

---

32   Gilles Kepel, *Jihad: The Trail of Political Islam*, translator Anthony F. Roberts (1st ed.) (Belknap Press of Harvard University Press, 2002), p. 72.

Frontier, bin Laden sought to perfect the new cult of 'jihad without borders', from which grew al Qaeda.

The extraordinary results of this contest were brought home to me by Dr Faud Hussein, chief of staff to President Barzani of Kurdistan, whom I met not far north of Baghdad. He told me:

> At Baghdad university in '67/'68 it was an individual relationship between you and God. Now it's a kind of shame if you don't go to the mosque.
>
> It's the difference between Marxism and communism. Like the Communist Party, the Islamists have become the vanguard of society. Here it is not a cult. It's the mass. My generation had secular ideologies. But the ideology of the left collapsed. The ideology of nationalism collapsed. Our nationalism is secular – but we're surrounded by a sea of Islamism … They believe in their cause. They are fighting not to love but to die. They're fighting against humanity. Not a country or a system. It's against humanity. Islamism is an ideology

of war; it's an ideology of hate; it's an ideology of destroying others.

The founders of the Islamic State, which emerged in the power vacuum left by the Allies' withdrawal from Iraq, shared much of the religious worldview of Osama bin Laden, but their political goals were much closer to the caliphate-building ambitions of 'political Islam' set out by writers such as Qutb.

When bin Laden and ISIS's founder, Abu Musab al-Zarqawi, first met in Afghanistan in 1996, bin Laden concluded that al-Zarqawi held 'rigid views' on religious doctrine.[33] It was soon clear that al-Zarqawi aspired to build more than an army; he thirsted for a complete social structure, saw Iraq as the place to start, and launched what was to become ISIS in 2003, only to die in a US air strike three years later. But in the maelstrom that followed America's

---

33 See *The Group that Calls Itself a State*, Combating Terrorism Center, op. cit.

exit from Iraq, ISIS emerged as the only force capable of providing governance and security to a Sunni population deeply alienated from the new Shi'ite-dominated government in Baghdad. As the group went from strength to strength, it announced in April 2013 a merger with Jabhat al-Nusra, one of the strongest Islamist forces opposing President Assad in Syria, and the foundation of Islamic State in Iraq and the Levant. Then, in June 2014, in a statement entitled 'This is God's promise', Abu Muhammad al-Adnani declared the 'proclamation of the establishment of the Islamic caliphate', under the leadership of Abu Bakr al-Baghdadi.

The history of ISIS's roots helps explain just why the extremism we face today is so hard to fight. But one thing is crystal clear: for nearly a century, the absolute core of the Islamists' argument is that there is a 'clash of civilisations' between Islam and the West.

In 'Towards the Light', written almost a century ago, Hassan al-Banna wrote that Egypt was at a cross-roads. One way, he wrote, led to 'the way of Islam, its fundamental assumptions, its principles, its culture, and its civilisation; the second is the way of the West … It is our belief that the first way, the way of Islam, its principles and its fundamental assumptions, is the only way that ought to be followed.'[34] 'We assert', he went on, 'that the civilisation of the west … is now bankrupt and in decline. Its foundations are crumbling, and its institutions and guiding principles are falling apart.'[35] This was not so far away from the sentiment of the new 'Caliph' proclamations that the day was coming 'when a Muslim will walk everywhere as a master'.

For a century, Islamist extremists have contended that the West and Islam are locked in an epic battle to predominate. And the problem with our conduct in the battle of ideas today is that too many Western politicians are not contesting the argument. They are agreeing with it.

---

34   Euben and Zaman, op. cit., p. 37.

35   Euben and Zaman, ibid., p. 58.

CHAPTER 3

WINNING THE BATTLE OF IDEAS

The Western argument that we are locked in a clash of civilisations emerged in the work of American historian Bernard Lewis, an adviser to George W. Bush, who coined the phrase in an article in 1990 entitled 'The Roots of Muslim Rage: Why So Many Muslims Deeply Resent the West, and Why Their Bitterness Will Not Be Easily Mollified'.

The concept was then popularised by the academic Samuel Huntingdon, in his 1993 *Foreign Affairs* article, 'The Clash of Civilizations', which argued:

'the fundamental source of conflict in this new world will not be primarily ideological or primarily economic. The great divisions among humankind and the dominating source of conflict will be cultural.'

The idea of a world war between an Islamic worldview and a 'Western-liberal' worldview has proved deeply influential in Conservative circles, inspiring both an attack on 'multiculturalism' and the idea of a 'conveyor belt' that leads people from conservative Islamic belief to anti-Western violence.

Unfortunately, when many Muslims hear ministers attack 'Islamism', it sounds awfully similar to an attack on 'Islam'. When politicians use phrases such as 'political Islam' or 'Islamist' or 'extreme Muslim' the risk is that an attack on some sounds like an attack on every Muslim in the country. What is meant as an attack on heretics sounds like an attack on the faithful. The conduct of this debate makes many British Muslims feel like their faith is under siege.

If we want to isolate our enemies, we have to snap any chance of an alliance between them and their own citizens. So politicians' rhetoric is not helping. The conduct of Donald Trump is a warning. In the wake of the San Bernardino shootings in California, Mr Trump said he wanted 'a total and complete shutdown of Muslims entering the United States until our country's representatives can figure out what the hell is going on'.

Within days, the terrorist group Al Shabaab released a video[36] packaged around the video clip of the late Anwar al-Awlaki, who was killed in September 2011.

'Muslims of the West,' it warned, 'take heed and learn from the lessons of history; there are ominous clouds gathering in your horizon. Yesterday, America was a land of slavery, segregation, lynching and Ku Klux Klan and tomorrow it will be a land of religious discrimination and concentration camps.

'The west will eventually turn against its Muslim citizens, hence, my advice to you is this: you have

---

36 Al Shabaab uses Donald Trump in video aimed at Western Muslims, www.edition.cnn.com/2016/01/02/middleeast/ al-shabaab-video-trump/

two choices – either hijra or jihad. You either leave or you fight.'

*　*　*

I think there is a way to win the battle of ideas without falling into the trap of divide and rule set for us by our enemies. But it took a visit to the refugee camps of northern Iraq for me to see it.

The road east from Erbil takes you through the beautiful, sharp, limestone ridges of the Zagros mountains, the thousand-mile range as old as the Alps, which divides the Iranian Plateau from the rich flood-plains of Mesopotamia. Once home to Neanderthals, it was here that early settlers pioneered wine-making, and today the ancestors of wheat, barley, lentils, almonds, walnuts, pistachios and pomegranates can still be found growing wild, along with the remnants of the Persian oaks that once carpeted the slopes.

The road winds up through valleys cut by streams

and ice, through the rough, rubbly fields hewed from the deep brown moutainside and spotted with sage green oak trees. These mountains are sacred to the Kurds, and along the road you see the rhythms of a mountain life that hasn't changed much for centuries: young boys shepherding goats, a family stretched out in the sun on a tarpaulin picnicking by a stream, the roadside butchers' sheds with carcasses strung up in the cool mountain air.

We were headed for the Ashti camp, outside Sulaymaniyah. Escorted by the governor, who was once a doctor in Kingston upon Thames, we swept in and sat down in a giant, hot plastic tent to hear from dads and granddads dressed in traditional Arab dress, of the horror that brought them to Ashti.

A fine old man, proud and tough, told us of his tragedy: 'We've never hated anyone. We've never hurt anyone. But we can't go home until it's safe.' Some had lost wives and children as they fled across the surging waters of the river Tigris. The camp's Yazidi leader pleaded with us to highlight ISIS's capture of thousands of Yazidi wives and daughters, raped, enslaved and now bought and sold in ISIS markets for £100 each. Something that strikes you instantly in refugee camps is a simple truth: they're full of parents trying to save their children. As one man put it to me, 'Our life is our children.'

Over a hundred miles west, in the Baharka camp in Erbil, I heard similar tales. Here are thousands of Sunni Arabs, Kurds and Palestinians who fled last year when ISIS stormed Mosul, a mixed city of three million people.

The camp's managers explained, 'Lots of people here once had everything. They had houses, flat-screen TVs, good jobs. At the last minute, they had to flee. They grabbed their kids, got in cars and drove as fast as they could.' One hundred thousand people left in one night, jamming the roads out of the city. Now they're empty-handed. 'When they run away,' explained the camp manager, 'they run away with nothing.'

In one of the white tents, emblazoned with the

blue insignia of the United Nations, I met Ahmed and his five beautiful little kids. The tent was warm, with a sort of felt on the ground, and cushions and battered, dirty, turquoise cuddly bunnies and teddy bears scattered around, for the children. I don't think I'll ever forget their faces. Ahmed told me how he trekked hundreds of miles through the mountains with his tiny children – all under nine – and lost everything along the way. His mum and dad were still in Mosul. He didn't know if they were alive or dead. 'The reality of life under ISIS,' he said, 'is that it's no life at all.'

Throughout the camp, children were doing what children do all around the world. In their little wellies and flip-flops, printed dresses and grubby Barcelona FC tops, they were playing on battered bikes, pushing green and red plastic toy diggers and trucks through piles of mud, kicking a ball around a stony football pitch. Outside a caravan, dirty toddlers were playing in the stream of water pouring from a broken pipe. The older kids stood and gawped at our guards with their machine guns slung casually over their backs. Their parents were running out of hope, desperate to get back home.

And amid the horror, it suddenly struck me.

Nearly everyone in these camps were Muslims.

The fight against extremism is not a clash of civilisations. It is a clash *within* a civilisation – the oldest civilisation on earth.

I know from my work in Birmingham just how hard it is to get different mosques to work together. When I get a bit irritated with people not pulling together, I sometimes get told, 'Oh, please don't make us work with our enemies' – by which they mean the mosque down the road. Politics has divided the Middle East region since the authors of ancient clay tablets captured for posterity the arguments between the Akkadians and Sumerians two thousand years before Christ. And what you see glaring in the hot sun of Kurdistan is the simple truth: that Islam is a religion as diverse as any other world faith, and, therefore, just as divided.

Today, Islam is being torn apart by an age-old religious struggle to define what is orthodox and what is heresy, and a second, newer conflict: a political battle between the tyranny of theocracy and the freedom to plot one's own personal path to paradise. What is at stake is something worth fighting for. Yes, it is a war to defeat ISIS's aspirant empire of intolerance, but it is also, crucially, something more: a struggle to deliver freedom of conscience for 1.3 billion Muslims across the Islamic world and beyond, a group of our fellow citizens who may soon number one in five of the world's population.

Heretics always describe themselves as the true believers, and heretics always have scripture to draw on. Most holy books from the old days tend to be full of sex and violence. Take the Book of Samuel in the Bible. Here, God instructs King Saul to attack the Amalekites: 'And utterly destroy all that they have, and do not spare them ... kill both man and woman, infant and nursing child, ox and sheep, camel and donkey.' It is a prescription for genocide. When Saul failed to act, God took away his kingdom. Down the ages, Popes have variously declared Muslims and Protestants to be Amalekites and therefore right for destruction.[37]

Today, ISIS or al Qaeda-inspired attacks make up a very small slice of political violence. Over the past five years in Europe, only 2 per cent of terrorist attacks were committed by so-called Muslims. Europol notes that the vast majority of terror attacks in Europe are perpetrated by separatist groups or right-wing nationalists. Fanatics of many persuasions try to use the language or symbology of Christianity to justify violence; there is, for instance, the US-based Army of God, which promotes killing abortion providers and which boasts a significant number of its members in American jails for murder. There is the violent Chinese Christian group, Eastern Lightning. There's the Lord's

---

37 For a longer discussion, see NPR's 'Is the Bible More Violent Than the Quran?', http://www.npr.org/templates/story/story. php?storyId=124494788

Resistance Army, founded in Uganda, which has committed thousands of murders and kidnappings. There's the Phineas Priesthood, which emerged from the US Christian Identity movement, and was also involved in abortion clinic bombings. It was heavily influenced by the Ku Klux Klan, which, let's not forget, announce their presence with flaming crosses. Generally speaking, most religions down the centuries profit from prophets, scholars and gurus who pinpoint the 'trumps' in scripture. Wise people winnow out 'correct interpretation', re-asserting the calls to live a life of peace, harmony and being nice to the neighbours. By common consent, ISIS proposes a heretical creed; but it is acting like a killer virus trying to wipe out the glorious diversity of Islam and replace it with a single, narrow, uniform, universal sect. In the West, we attack 'Islamists', when in fact our enemies are a narrow brand of heretics.

Now, some say 'it is not for us to judge who is the heretic in a religion that is not ours'. Actually, on this matter, we can take refuge in what has become the overwhelmingly theological opinion. The bottom line was elegantly laid out by a group of British Muslims in a fatwa reported on Sunday 31 August 2014. Endorsed by six senior UK Islamic scholars, including the Secretary General of the World Islamic Mission and Sheikh Moulana Muhammad Shahid Raza OBE, the executive secretary of the UK Muslim Law Shariah Council, the fatwa declared, 'IS is a heretical, extremist organisation and it is religiously prohibited to support or join it; furthermore it is an obligation on British Muslims to actively oppose its poisonous ideology.'[38] This could not be clearer.

ISIS's galaxy of theological error has been neatly summarised in a brilliant short book by Shaykh Muhammad Al-Yaqoubi,[39] but at the absolute core of

---

38 See Fatwa on the So-called 'Islamic State' (Formerly 'Islamic State in Iraq & Syria'), available at http://www.thesundaytimes.co.uk/sto/multimedia/archive/01091/Fatwa_on_ISIS_1091394a.pdf

39 See Shaykh Muhammad Al-Yaqoubi, *Refuting ISIS: A Rebuttal of Its Religious and Ideological Foundations* (Sacred Knowledge, 2015).

it, there are two key errors on which extremists rely: the first is that it is OK to kill others, and the second is that it is OK to kill yourself.

The idea that you can kill others whom you deem non-believers or 'apostates' is the concept of *takfir*. As a global group of 122 Islamic scholars put it in an open letter to ISIS's leader: 'This issue is of the upmost importance because it is used to justify the spilling of Muslim blood, violating their sanctity and usurping their wealth and rights.'[40]

Today, extremists adopt a vast definition of *takfir*, using it to excommunicate anyone who fails to embrace their interpretation of the faith. The basic position of Islam, however, the trump in the pack, is that murder is simply not acceptable. Scholars therefore underline a simple point: 'The slaying of a soul – any soul – is Haraam (forbidden and inviolable under Islamic law)' and so is committing a murder:

---

40 See Council on American–Islamic Relations (CAIR) and the Fiqh Council of North America, http://www.lettertobaghdadi.com/14/english-v14.pdf.

'If anyone slays a person, it would be as if he slew the whole people.'[41]

Scholars warn that accusing others of polytheism is absolutely not on: 'The Prophet warned against accusing people of polytheism and of taking up the sword against them: the person I fear for you the most is the man who has read the Quran … cast it off and thrown it behind him, and taken up the sword against his neighbour and accused him of polytheism.'[42]

As such, many leading Islamic scholars argue that ISIS is simply the modern incarnation of an old tradition in the Middle East sect known as the Khawarij, which appeared in the first century of Islam and became renowned for killing Muslims for alleged 'apostasy'. They were, said the Prophet, 'the worst of both men and animals' and as such, fighting ISIS 'is

---

41   Ibid., based on the Quranic verse, Surah Al-Ma'idah, 5:32.

42   Council on American–Islamic Relations (CAIR) and the Fiqh Council of North America, ibid., p. 9.

a legal obligation for those in the region in order to dismantle their criminal entity'.[43]

Just for good measure, the scholars added that any declarations made by a so-called apostate cannot be taken at face value 'without questioning or testing their faith', the intentions behind any such action must be known, it is forbidden to render a conclusion on someone's faith when there is a difference of opinion among Muslims scholars, and it is forbidden to declare any entire group – such as the Shi'ites – non-Muslim.[44] Oh, and the Quran is very clear that Muslims are not allowed to launch attacks on the societies in which they happen to live. And you certainly cannot go around creating *Lord of the Flies*-style dystopian chaos, where people like the Yazidis are slaughtered or sold into sexual slavery, where prisoners are decapitated, where civilians are massacred, not least because it is a violation of international treaties such as the Geneva

---

43   See Shaykh Muhammad Al-Yaqoubi, op. cit.

44   Ibid., p. 10.

Convention and the Prophet was very clear in the Quran: 'Believers, fulfil your covenants!'

The second key heresy is the idea that it's OK to go around killing yourself in pursuit of your ends. Extremists try to justify suicide as 'seeking martyrdom' on the basis that, in the Hadith, the companions of Muhammad were rewarded for 'throwing himself into the enemy's army alone … even if he knows that he would be killed'.[45] But the edicts against suicide bombing are very clear. First, there is the general prohibition on killing non-combatants, such as civilians. As the Quran puts it: 'Slay not the life which Allah has made sacrosanct unless it be in a just cause', and further, 'whoever kills a believer intentionally, his recompense is Hell to abide therein, and the Wrath and the Curse of Allah are upon him, and a great punishment is prepared for him'. As no one can say for sure 'this person is not a believer', it becomes forbidden to kill any human being without

---

45   See *Inspire* magazine, winter 2013.

just cause. Suicide itself is specifically prohibited in the edicts, 'Kill yourselves not, for Allah is truly merciful to you' and 'Throw not yourselves into the mouth of danger'.[46]

The stories of life under ISIS give us all the evidence we need to prove its heresy: the barbarism, the sham justice, the distinctly un-Quranic intolerance. This is a regime guilty of the genocide of the Yazidis; a regime whose leader keeps sex slaves and where sons execute their own mothers for religious crimes. Yet, despite its heresy, the ISIS project is to enforce this cult on a population of 1.1 billion Muslims, eliminating the extraordinary diversity of the world's Islamic faith. And here's the proof: ISIS and al Qaeda's victims are overwhelmingly Muslim. Al Qaeda has killed seven times more Muslims than non-Muslims.[47]

---

46 See, for instance, http://www.islamicsupremecouncil.org/ understanding-islam/legal-rulings/21-jihad-classical-islamic-perspective.html?start=14

47 See Counterterrorism Center at US Military Academy at West Point, 2009.

In the five years running up to 2011, the US National Counterterrorism Center found Muslims suffered between 82 and 97 per cent of terrorism-related fatalities. And in January 2016, the United Nations reported that ISIS was the 'prime actor' in 19,000 Iraqi deaths between January 2014 and October 2015.[48] There are few better illustrations of just what that tyranny would entail than the tragic story of Mosul.

Mosul stands 250 miles north of Baghdad, on the west bank of the Tigris River, across from the ancient Assyrian city of Nineveh. Once a diverse city of over two million people, it was occupied by ISIS in 2014. Its devastating story was set out for me one night in a battered office block in northern Iraq, where I met some very brave researchers who had been tracking the sentiment of Mosul residents throughout the ISIS era. At the firm's headquarters, the team described just how sentiment had changed over the months.

---

48 CNN, 'Nearly 19,000 Civilians Killed in Iraq in 21 Month Period', 19 January 2016.

The truth is that, at first, many residents welcomed ISIS – in fact, when the Iraqi security forces left, they were stoned in their Humvees by residents who had felt humiliated by their presence. But women hated the newcomers – in particular, they hated being told what to wear. The freedom to smoke was much constrained. New preachers were placed in the mosques. Despite all this, the prevailing view was that 'ISIS are basically reasonable people'. Soon, however, living standards were falling, and public violence rising. Mobile phone coverage was cut. Food prices rose. Electricity supplies became sporadic. Residents grew restless.

'Once you've tasted death,' said one resident, explaining the ISIS regime, 'you want to have the fever again.' The 'micro-management of religion treats people like children,' said another. Residents began to describe life as living in a prison. Asked to draw pictures of their lives, they drew crosses over their mouths, or drew themselves in cages. The regime began to sicken people with its obsessive control of the way everyone lived and prayed

– down to how men must style their beards – with brutal punishments for anyone stepping out of line.

This is the way that ISIS would seek to destroy the glorious diversity of the Muslim world, east and west, beyond the borders of the Middle East through to India and Pakistan and across north and central Africa.

It's worth reflecting on the sheer dimensions of the caliphate 'project': it is nothing less than a plan to roll up a total of sixty-seven nations, currently home to 2.6 billion people, including 1.1 billion Muslims, and impose upon it a Mosul-like regime of heretical intolerance.

Theologically, it is, of course, sheer nonsense. As a group of 122 imams declared, 'A new caliphate requires consensus from Muslims and not just from those in some small corner of the world … Announcing a caliphate without consensus is sedition because it renders the majority of Muslims who do not approve it outside of the caliphate.'[49]

---

49 See Council on American–Islamic Relations (CAIR) and the Fiqh
    Council of North America, op. cit., p. 15

So either Mr al-Baghdadi consulted the world's Muslims, of which there is precious little sign, or he decided that they're not Muslims. Indeed, the idea is so outrageous that even al Qaeda disagrees with it. As it happens, the Muslim population of Iraq and Syria is only 26.5 million people. So ISIS, controlling space that is home to perhaps 2 per cent of their projected caliphate, is declaring sovereignty over another 1.1 billion people. It's the equivalent of the leaders of Birmingham and the Black Country self-declaring sovereignty over the rest of the United Kingdom. Just like that.

Let's think of the diversity of the Muslim people across these lands that would simply be eliminated if ISIS were to succeed.

First, we have the basic divide between Sunni and Shi'ite, which dates back to within a few years of the prophet's death, and the Ibadi school followed in Oman. Mr al-Baghdadi has been very clear that he regards the Shi'ite not as Muslims, but as apostates. That would be a problem for the projected caliphate, because in at least five countries, including Iran, the majority of the population is Shi'ite, divided between some three different schools of jurisprudence. Indeed, in sub-Saharan Africa, south-eastern Europe and central Asia, Sunni Muslims are in the minority.

Second, within the Sunni tradition, there are at least five schools of thought – the Hanafi, Maliki, Shafi'i, Hanbali and Ẓāhirī traditions – and within these there are many subdivisions. Wahhabis claim to follow the Hanbali school, but even within Wahhabism, it's possible to identify the quietist and activist traditions.

MEDIAN PERCENTAGE OF MUSLIMS IDENTIFYING AS SUNNI IN SELECTED REGIONS, 2008–12

South Asia	90%
South-east Asia	75%
Middle East and North Africa	67%
Sub-Saharan Africa	48%
South-eastern Europe	27%
Central Asia	21%

Source: Pew Research, The World's Muslims: Unity and Diversity, Religious Affiliation, August 2012.

DISTRIBUTION OF SCHOOLS OF ISLAMIC JURISPRUDENCE

Source: Re-orienting the veil, Islamic Jurisprudence and Law, accessed 15/01/2016. See the website for a full list of countries by largest denomination. *Map: Wikimedia Commons, Public Domain*

Third, across the Islamic world, there are many Muslims identifying as Sufi, a practice that emphasises an intense, interior search for perfection of worship. In some countries, such as Senegal and Chad, Sufis form the majority of the population. Again, this is not a tradition that ISIS or al Qaeda has much time for. As one expert notes, 'Salafis [the branch of Islam from which ISIS derives their heresy] have usually been unrelentingly hostile to devotional Sufi practices.' Indeed, the spiritual father of Salafi Islam, Muhammad ibn 'Abd al-Wahhab, was hostile not only to Shi'ism and to Sufi devotionalism, but also to 'anything he deemed not to be in strict conformity with the teachings of the foundational texts.'[50]

Now think about the diversity of *attitudes* across this vast region. The extraordinary pluralism of the world's Muslims shines through in the research on religion and public life undertaken by the Pew Research Centre.[51] In an incredible survey involving 38,000

---

50   See Euben and Zaman, op. cit., pp. 20–21

51   30 April 2013.

PERCENTAGE OF MUSLIMS IDENTIFYING AS SUFI
IN SELECTED COUNTRIES, 2008–2012

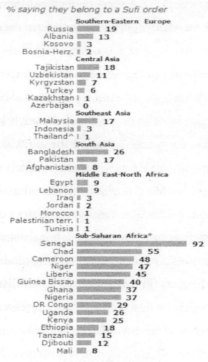

% saying they belong to a Sufi order

Southern-Eastern Europe
- Russia 19
- Albania 13
- Kosovo 3
- Bosnia-Herz. 2

Central Asia
- Tajikistan 18
- Uzbekistan 11
- Kyrgyzstan 7
- Turkey 6
- Kazakhstan 1
- Azerbaijan 0

Southeast Asia
- Malaysia 17
- Indonesia 3
- Thailand^ 1

South Asia
- Bangladesh 26
- Pakistan 17
- Afghanistan 8

Middle East-North Africa
- Egypt 9
- Lebanon 9
- Iraq 3
- Jordan 2
- Morocco 1
- Palestinian terr. 1
- Tunisia 1

Sub-Saharan Africa*
- Senegal 92
- Chad 55
- Cameroon 48
- Niger 47
- Liberia 45
- Guinea Bissau 40
- Ghana 37
- Nigeria 37
- DR Congo 29
- Uganda 26
- Kenya 25
- Ethiopia 18
- Tanzania 15
- Djibouti 12
- Mali 8

*Data for all countries except Niger from "Tolerance and
Tension: Islam and Christianity in Sub-Saharan Africa."
^Interviews conducted with Muslims in five southern
provinces only.

Source: Pew Research, The World's Muslims: Unity and Diversity,
Religious Affiliation, August 2012.

face-to-face interviews in over eighty languages, the Pew study surveys Muslims in thirty-nine countries. It is a remarkable cornucopia of attitudes.

One of the most important questions regards attitudes towards sharia law. In Afghanistan, 99 per cent of the Muslim population favours making sharia law the official law of the country. But in Lebanon, the figure falls to just 29 per cent, and indeed, across Central Asia – Kurdistan, Tajikistan, Turkey, Kazakhstan, Azerbaijan – only a very small minority favours making sharia the law of the land. In sub-Saharan Africa, there are big differences too. In Niger, 86 per cent of the population want sharia law – but that falls to just 37 per cent in Tanzania. In Turkey, home to one of the biggest Muslim populations in the world, just 12 per cent of Muslims favour making sharia the law of the land. Even among sharia supporters in south-eastern Europe, south Asia, central Asia, south-east Asia, the Middle East and north Africa, the majority believe it should apply only to Muslims.

Tens of millions of Muslims across the so-called

lands of the caliphate believe that their national identity is more important than their religious identity.
And the statistics show Muslims are united in the
rejection of violence in the name of Islam. As the
Pew study concludes, 'asked specifically about suicide bombing, clear majorities in most countries say
such acts are rarely or never justified as a means of
defending Islam from its enemies'.

What's more, in a majority of the countries
surveyed, at least half of Muslims say they are somewhat or very concerned about religious extremism.
In fact, most Muslims around the world say they
support democracy and most say that freedom of
religion is important: over 90 per cent of Muslims in
sub-Saharan Africa, south-east Asia, south-eastern
Europe, central Asia and south Asia say religious
freedom is a good thing.

So, what is crystal clear is that Islam is a faith of
beautiful diversity. It is a diversity that ISIS and al
Qaeda want to wipe out in order to impose a draco-
nian new dogma.

Some 1,600 years after the birth of Christianity, Europe was wracked by the brutal wars of religion between Catholics and Protestants.[52] In the blood-bath of the Thirty Years' War (1618–48), millions of Europeans were killed as a Roman Catholic Emperor sought to impose uniformity of faith across Protestant northern Europe. It was settled only with an edict of toleration establishing the parameters of what we now think of today as freedom of conscience.

Today, some 1,500 years after the birth of Islam, the Middle East is wracked by a division between those who want to impose a heretical theocracy and those democratically minded Muslims who want the freedom to fathom their own road to heaven. Rather than respect the 'dignity of difference', for the extremists the devil is in the diversity. ISIS and their allies don't want diversity. They want uniformity,

---

52   Indeed, the English puritans had very strong views on what Christian orthodoxy looked like, and strongly objected to Charles I's flavour of Protestant belief, known as Arminianism.

and they're prepared to kill their way there, creating not a path to heaven but to hell on earth.

This simple insight has crucial implications for how we frame our fight with extremists. What you see on the frontline in Iraq is that the fight we're waging is not between Islam and the West. The fight we're waging is against heresy – and tyranny. There is no clash of civilisations; there's a clash between the civilised and a cult. The 'civilised' are on the same side: we may be diverse, but we share an ambition to be free, to be faithful on our terms – not dictated to by totalitarian theocrats – however prone to error and weakness we, as mere mortals, might be.

THE FORK
IN THE ROAD

CHAPTER 4

THE FORK
IN THE ROAD

Sulaimaan is a big man of Somalian heritage with a Brummie accent, a fantastic smile and a down-to-earth manner. His job is one of the most important in the country. Sulaimaan is a mentor for the Channel programme, working with young people deemed at risk of 'radicalisation'. Sulaimaan's job is to interact with them, re-shape their worldview and bring them back to sanity. It's tough role, not least because some informal reports I've heard suggest half the young people referred have some sort of adolescent mental health issue.

I asked to meet some of Birmingham's Channel mentors at my Hodge Hill HQ to get a much clearer idea of just why young people get drawn into a world that, to most of us, seems a world apart. And what I was about to hear permanently changed my view of just how radicalisation works.

In the text books, 'radicalisation' is defined as 'a process of change, a personal and political transformation from one condition to another'.[53] We all go through changes on life's great journey, but for some young people today, that change shifts them into the path of violence.

I started by asking Sulaimaan what sort of young people he tended to meet. Smiling, he said:

Their issues are often about being powerless, feeling that they're being represented as the perpetrators. So they automatically reject the

---

53 Kris Christmann, 'Preventing Religious Radicalisation and Violent Extremism: A Systematic Review of the Research Evidence', Research Report, Youth Justice Board, 2012.

mainstream narrative and go online to search for what they feel is a true representation of themselves. What they find is a feeling that they're accepted there.

At the time they might have a problem with their community. They might not feel engaged with them. In other words they feel as if they're in a kind of no man's land. Online, they find the community where they feel at home.

They're often lost in terms of faith as a source of strength, because they can't relate to scholars and leaders – let's be honest, many of them are from villages or live in an isolated world. So they revert to the internet and latch onto preachers who appeal to them.

Some people have little contact with their faith. But they grew up in a house that was culturally Muslim. They might have had a British education, moved up the ladder and got into the system and then found barriers that they have to overcome that perhaps others don't.

Like millions of people worldwide, these young people are stumbling over a search for meaning – and often, there is great frustration in their lives. Suddenly they find a sense of purpose that is open to them, which they simply cannot see in the media's representation of the world around them. Sulaimaan went on:

> As the media awakens their identity, they just hear that they're one part of this wicked and cruel religion. For others it's all about finding a sense of purpose. If I'm told I don't belong here then I'm open to finding an alternative identity elsewhere. A lot of people ask themselves how long do you have to live in Britain before you become part of the majority? But people are often looking at the Quran not necessarily as a theological argument but rather a way of life.
>
> Online, young people find in radical preachers the purpose they feel is missing in life around them.

In the mosque, the ideal of social justice often isn't there. If you go to the madrassa it's often just rote learning. But there's nothing about *why* they do this from the imam. But [the extremists offer] an emotional appeal. People want to think they're acting patriotically and think 'I am willing to sacrifice to something. And here is how I can contribute violently.'

In the space of an hour, Sulaimaan demystified for me some of the most perplexing stories I've read: the backstories of those who go from the banality of normality to commit the most unspeakable atrocities.

Take the story of Thomas Evans, one of the first British citizens killed fighting for the East African Islamist extremist group Al Shabaab. The six-foot happy-go-lucky Manchester United fan grew up in High Wycombe, was a cute kid full of energy and mischief who liked chasing magpies in the garden. He grew into a teenager who loved heavy metal and drinking in local pubs, and professed that his first ambition was to join the Royal Marines 'to serve my country'. He wasn't the most tolerant of boys. His dad said that the teenage Thomas was vocal about his dislike of 'Pakis'. When he lost his job and his long-term girlfriend, he converted to Islam, became devout, hung out with new friends and, in 2011, fled the country to Egypt and then Kenya. There, he was linked to attacks in south-east Kenya in which more than ninety people were murdered. His poor mother told *The Times*, 'If a young man from High Wycombe raised in a secular household can be turned into a terrorist, then perhaps no one is immune.'

Or think about 'Abu Basir al-Britani', who became a media star for al Qaeda-linked Jabhat al-Nusra, waving AK-47s in propaganda videos. He turned out to be Lucas Kinney, the British son of Hollywood film director Patrick Kinney, who helped direct *Braveheart* and *Rambo: First Blood*. Lucas was born in Hammer-smith, enjoyed drinking and played guitar in a rock band called Hannah's Got Herpes.

Then there's Sana Ahmed, sentenced to twenty-five years in December 2015 for helping her husband – nicknamed 'the Silent Bomber' – prepare huge bombs. She was the daughter of a magistrate. The stories of normality giving way to extremism go on and on.

The challenge for the security services today is stark: there is no single individual profile that helps us pinpoint who is most at risk of becoming a terrorist – and certainly nothing that helps us understand precisely *when* someone might be about to become bloody dangerous.

Biological theories end up simply underlining the age-old truth that young men between their early teens and mid-twenties are quite risky. Psychological theories (psychopathology, personality traits, repressed sexuality) have not got much further. And the 'it's all society's fault' theory does not seem to work either, given that so many terrorists have nice, middle-class backgrounds.

We do now understand the 'risk factors' a little better. The problem is, there are loads of them.

MI5 first set out the 'key vulnerabilities'[54] back in 2008, and over the past eight years, 'models' have evolved. One such model includes twenty-eight items.[55] Ten issues relate to 'attitude' (e.g. attachment to an ideology justifying violence, perception of injustice and grievances, and identity problems) another five relate to context (e.g. use of extremist websites or direct contact with violent extremists); six relate to personal history of violence; five questions relate to whether the individual confronts barriers to violence (e.g. have they chosen a political path to change instead?); and three relate to personal circumstances (sexual orientation, marriage, age). In other words, it's all

---

54 See report 'Understanding Radicalisation and Violent Extremism in the UK' (2008). The MI5 list included marginalisation and racism consequent upon the experience of migrating to Britain; a past criminal record; the failure to make career advances despite holding university degrees; contact with extremist networks overseas; and religious naivety.

55 D. Elaine Pressman, 'Risk Assessment Decisions for Violent Political Extremism', October 2009. I thank Harvey Redgrave for the reference.

very complicated, it's very hard to predict who is going to become a terrorist – and we certainly can't predict when.

VIOLENT EXTREMISM:

FIFTEEN WELL-KNOWN RISK FACTORS

Cultural or religious isolation from family

Risk-taking behaviours

Sudden changes in religious practice

Violent rhetoric

Negative peer influences

Isolation from peer group

Use of hate rhetoric

Use of death rhetoric

Political activism

Basic paramilitary training

Travel or residence abroad

Membership of an extremist group

Contact with known recruiters/extremists

Advanced paramilitary training

Overseas combat

So, can we really say what drives young men and women to violence?

Well, David Cameron had a theory. Indeed, he had become, among other things, advocate-in-chief of what's called the 'conveyor belt' theory of extremism. The conveyor belt theory draws a *direct line* between extremist or ultra-orthodox religious views and terrorist violence. It is a sort of outworking of the 'Clash of Civilisations' argument.

The formal definition of the theory goes like this: there is 'a consistent and predictable progression from the adoption of religiously conservative views as a response to political alienation, to involvement in or support for terrorism'. It suggests that 'the path to terrorism has a fixed trajectory and that each step of the process has specific, identifiable markers'.

The theory proposes four basic stages, and reflects a simplistic and now discredited model first proposed by the New York Police Department.[56] The first

---

56 See Faiza Patel, 'Rethinking Radicalization', Brennan Center for Justice, 2011, p. 14. The NYPD study used limited data and a faulty methodology of ten hand-picked case studies.

stage is when the individual is exposed to jihadi ideology. The second stage is 'self-identification', when
the individual shifts from his or her old identity and
begins associating with those who hold extremist views. The third stage is indoctrination, when
the experience is intensified and an extremist ideology adopted. Crucially, at this stage, the individual
buys into the idea that further action is required.
At the final stage, the individual accepts a duty to
support or participate in terrorist activities and 'self-
designates' as a holy warrior.

The theory's virtue is that it's nice and simple,
with the comforting idea that an individual can
be prevented from turning to terrorism if the process of radicalisation can be disrupted in its early
stages by law enforcement agents trained to look for
the right signs. David Cameron liked the idea a lot.
In his speech to the Munich Security Conference in
February 2011, he declared that 'as evidence emerges
about the backgrounds of those convicted of terrorist offences, it is clear that many of them were

initially influenced by what some have called "non-violent extremists'". He underlined the point in his statement to the House of Commons following the murder of Lee Rigby:

> For some young people, it is as if there is a conveyor belt to radicalisation that has poisoned their minds with sick and perverted ideas. We need to dismantle that process at every stage – in schools, colleges and universities, on the internet, in our prisons and wherever it takes place…

Finally, in Birmingham, in July 2015, he added:

> No one becomes a terrorist from a standing start … It may begin with hearing about the so-called Jewish conspiracy and then develop into hostility to the West and fundamental liberal values, before finally becoming a cultish attachment to death. Put another way, the extremist

worldview is the gateway, and violence is the ultimate destination.

The theory inspired much of the government's approach set out in the Counter-Extremism Strategy published in October 2015, in which the former Prime Minister said, 'We know that terrorism is really a symptom; ideology is the root cause.'

There is only one problem with the conveyor belt theory. And that is that it's wrong.

Three organisations that know quite a lot about the process of radicalisation are the FBI, the CIA and MI5. Over the years, experts from all three organisations have gone on the record setting out their worldview.

In its seminal research, 'Understanding Radicalisation and Violent Extremism in the UK', leaked to *The Guardian* in 2008, MI5 concluded that there is no single pathway to extremism. In fact, in a study of several hundred individuals, it found that all had taken strikingly different journeys to violent extremist activity. The work inspired a British civil service report on non-violent extremists, which concluded that 'we do not believe that it is accurate to regard radicalisation in this country as a linear "conveyor belt" moving from grievance, through radicalisation, to violence ... This thesis seems to both misread the radicalisation process and to give undue weight to ideological factors.'

Joe Navarro is one of the founding members of the FBI's Behavioral Analysis Program. He was once asked: 'In your study of terrorism and those who commit lone-wolf attacks, have you found universal factors that guide their actions?' His answer was fascinating:

> The one thing we know is that the psychology has always been the same. By that, I mean you have individuals who are collecting wounds, they're looking for social ills, or things that have gone wrong, and they are nourishing these things that they're ideating, that they're thinking about. The solution for them is violence. The psychology is always the same.

Marc Sageman is a forensic psychiatrist and former CIA case officer who has studied more than 500 terrorists. He too concludes the conveyor belt theory simply is not accurate. 'One cannot simply draw a line,' he says, 'put markers on it, engage with people who are along this path to see whether they are close to committing atrocities.'[57]

Sageman proposes an alternative four-stage model of al Qaeda-influenced radicalisation. It begins not with 'religious conservatism', but with a sense of 'moral outrage'; it evolves as the individual develops a specific interpretation of the world (for instance, where moral violations are seen as representing a 'war against Islam'); somehow, there is then a resonance with personal experiences; and finally, the individual is mobilised through recruitment networks.

This unfortunate reality is confirmed by more and more frontline police and academic experience,

---

57 Marc Sageman, *Leaderless Jihad* (University of Pennsylvania Press, 2008), quoted in *The Guardian*, 9 June 2011.

and what is becoming very clear is that the starting point for radicalisation may in fact be rage rather than religion – and social networks may be far more important than we thought. In other words, it's not your madrassa that is the problem, it's your mates.

Let's take a look first at the role of religion.

The 2008 MI5 study concluded that, 'far from being religious … a large number of those involved in terrorism do not practise their faith regularly'. A good illustration came back in 2012, when five men were arrested travelling to attack an English Defence League demonstration in Dewsbury. They were stopped and found to be transporting a home-made bomb made out of a firework, containing 359 nails and ninety-three ball bearings, along with two sawn-off shotguns, parts of other explosive devices, knives and a long printed message, dated the same day, describing their motivation and calling the Queen a 'female devil'. But according to a West Midlands Police counter-terrorism expert I spoke to, they were at best 'religious novices'.

The case underlines the problem, that it is always risky taking self-proclaimed motives at face value when you might be hearing merely a well-rehearsed rationale used to justify completely unacceptable behaviour. This points to a second danger: young people effectively constructing their own religion to justify violence.

Many young people struggle with the big questions in life: Why am I here? What's the meaning of it all? But instead of popping along to the mosque or the imam for answers, they research online and create their own 'DIY Islam', facilitated by the nice people they meet in extremist chatrooms.

Perhaps the most notorious example was the case of school friends Yusuf Sarwar and Mohammed Ahmed, two Birmingham men who were convicted of fighting in Syria. At their trial, it emerged that they had ordered online copies of *Islam for Dummies* before they left.

This phenomenon could help explain why perhaps as many as a quarter of terrorism offences have been perpetrated not by people brought up as Muslims, but by converts, including the notorious 'Jihadi Sid', the East Ender who was filmed brutally murdering five Syrians in an ISIS propaganda video, who converted to Islam from Buddhism, of all things. Indeed, experts now conclude that 'a well-developed Muslim identity actually counteracts jihadism'.[58]

A number of international cases all now underline the importance of rage over religion. One journalist, who for six months infiltrated an ISIS cell planning a terrorist attack in France, known as 'Soldiers of Allah', reported that he found 'lost, frustrated, suicidal, easily manipulated youths'. He 'never saw any Islam',[59] but what he did find was a very dangerous ring-leader, a former Satanist and alcoholic, who was furious that he had been turned down by the French army.

---

58 Faiza Patel, op. cit., p. 8

59 'Journalist Who Infiltrated Isis Cell Planning a Terror Attack in France "Never Saw Any Islam"', *Independent*, 3 May 2016.

Aydin Soei, a Danish sociologist, offers another example. He met Omar Abdel Hamid El-Hussein, the gunman of the Copenhagen shootings on 14 and 15 February 2015. '[El-Hussein]', he said, 'wasn't an intellectual Islamist with a long beard … This was a loser.'[60]

The bottom line is that there is now plenty of evidence that suggests the road to violence *does not* start with religious extremism, or religious practice, or religious commitment. Indeed, religious practice appears, if anything, to be an antidote to violence and helps glue diverse communities together.[61]

Different evidence is emerging from studies of the so-called Foreign Fighters Phenomenon. Among the most expert are the team at King's College London, led by Professor Peter Neumann, who came to the House of Commons recently to brief MPs.

---

60 'Anger of Suspect in Danish Killings Is Seen as Only Loosely Tied to Islam', *New York Times*, 16 February 2015.

61 I thank my friend Stephen Timms MP for this point. His constituency, Newham, has a low number of people self-reporting as of 'no faith' on the census, and while diverse, is cohesive.

Fascinating patterns are emerging from their database of the hundreds of British nationals who have gone to fight in Syria and Iraq, and when ISIS's recruitment records were leaked to Sky News, it provided a new opportunity to confirm what is known as the 'bunch of guys' theory of radicalisation: the idea that social networks are fundamental to recruitment patterns.[62]

We can now see links between the twenty to thirty original 'entrepreneurs' who went to fight in the Levant and the social networks that connected them to the hundreds that followed. So, while ISIS skilfully exploited social media to spread their message of hate, real-world connections turned out to be fundamental to actually mobilising people. Analysis of the leaked recruitment records revealed many British fighters arriving in groups and often from

---

62 Clare Ellis and Raffaello Pantucci, 'Friends, Sponsors and Bureaucracy: An Initial Look at the Daesh Database'. See https://rusi.org/commentary/friends-sponsors-and-bureaucracy-initial-look-daesh-database

the same place, in particular Coventry, Cardiff and Portsmouth. In other words, once again, your mates are far more important than your madrassa.

So, it's all quite complicated. How do we make sense of it all? To try and get a better handle on the best current thinking, I sat down with some front-line intelligence experts to hear what they had to say. And what is clear is that while there may not be a single terrorist profile, and while there are lots of different 'models',[63] there are now some quite recognisable dynamics.

First, there is the personal – what are often called the 'push factors'. This might include a dysfunctional family. It might include some sort of crisis, a lack of integration, grievances or an element of criminality. These factors all add up to the same psychological

---

63 For instance: the Prevent Pyramid (The Association of Chief Police Officers, 2007), the New York Police Department's four-stage radicalisation process (NYPD, 2007); Sageman's four-stage model (Sageman, 2007); and Taarnby's eight-stage recruitment process (Taarnby, 2005) to name just a few. I am grateful to Harvey Redgrave for the references.

effect, clearing out the obstacles to getting involved in violence.

The second stage, which may overlap with the first, involves the 'pull' factors or 'radicalising influences'. These might arise as a result of a family member being mixed up in terrorism or extremism; the influences could also come from close friends, or a radicaliser.

Some people have the misfortune to grow up in families harbouring elements of extremism. Often, however, a radicaliser will be found at a university or in a prison. In some high-security jails, such as Long Lartin in Worcestershire, Muslims now make up 40 per cent of the mainstream population, among whom are prisoners with extremist views who are pressuring non-Muslims to convert to Islam.

Of course, the radicaliser is now more often found on the internet. For online influences to work, however, there has to be an absence of obstacles, and, vitally, a *'switch'*. The 'switch' typically required to move someone to the dark side is some kind of 'shock' or an 'ideological opening'. It could be a single event, or it could be exposure to a particular cause, but the crucial point is that it provides a connection to meaning, and in the case of ISIS and al Qaeda, this meaning is expressed as a redemptive conflict through which the individual can find some kind of virtue or redemption by joining.

Look for instance at one classic appeal made by Osama bin Laden: 'We pray to God that He will open the way for them to wreak revenge on the Jews and the Americans. *Some countries have ordered us to stop attacking America, but we believe these attacks are a duty incumbent upon us.*[64] [My italics]' In 2004, bin Laden underlined the point in a message addressed to the American people: 'We have been fighting you ... just as you violate our security, so we violate yours.'

Now listen to how that basic call was mimicked in the infamous last will and testament of Mohammad

---

64 Quoted in Thomas Hegghammer and Petter Nesser, 'Assessing the Islamic State's Commitment to Attacking the West', http://www.terrorismanalysts.com/pt/index.php/pot/article/view/440/html

Sidique Khan, one of the 7/7 bombers, whose video statement was aired on the Arabic television channel Al Jazeera after his death. The focus of the video is the perceived injustice against Muslims with which Khan justified violence in retaliation:

> Your democratically elected governments continuously perpetuate atrocities against my people all over the world. And your support of them makes you directly responsible, just as I am directly responsible for protecting and avenging my Muslim brothers and sisters.
>
> Until we feel security, you will be our targets. And until you stop the bombing, gassing, imprisonment and torture of my people, we will not stop this fight. We are at war and I am a soldier.

Once someone is through the ideological opening, the radicalisation process will then typically involve joining a group – real or virtual – and a deepening commitment before violent behaviour.

This reality underlines just why the 'conveyor belt' theory is so risky. Not only does it inaccurately describe what is actually happening, but worse, it leads politicians into taking steps that help reinforce the 'clash of civilisations' argument that al Qaeda and ISIS use as 'the ideological switch' to inspire young recruits that 'Islam is under attack'. This is why the theory was rejected by experts such as Marc Sageman, who argued in May 2013 that the theory was 'the same nonsense that led governments a hundred years ago to claim that left-wing political protests led to violent anarchy'.

Worse, the theory is now inspiring governments to marginalise religion in public life, which only seeks to confirm the extremists' argument that Islam is under assault. If you believe that religious conservatism is the root cause of violent behaviour, then before long, you end up with politicians trying to regulate private religious practice or education, for example, regulating private faith education. And there is a particular risk that politicians end up being seen not to attack 'Islamism' but Islam itself.

One of the best speakers I have heard on this is not a Muslim activist, but a Christian Conservative Member of Parliament, Fiona Bruce MP. Fiona recently put to a meeting of the Commons a simple point, that today we have 'Ofsted inspectors making a judgement as to whether my religious beliefs are good or not'. Ms Bruce points out that she is a creationist. 'Does that', she asks, 'make me an extremist? And if not, who says so?' If rights to religious freedom are not preserved, then will other rights soon suffer? The reality is that in many diverse communities, faith can act as a kind of glue, helping the business of integration.

Given a choice between, on the one side, Channel mentors such as Sulaimaan, our Security Services and academic experts like Shiraz Maher and Marc Sageman on the one hand, and the former Prime Minister on the other, I know who I would side with.

But I am not interested in simply knocking down the government's thesis. I'm searching for the right explanation for the process. Intelligence experts describe to me a process that they call 'snakes and ladders'. Certain kinds of experiences, like ladders, take young people closer to violence. But, then something might happen, like landing on a snake, that takes them backwards. It's not a process we understand terribly well.

For me, the best explanation emerged not from books or reports, but in a conversation with some frontline faith leaders.

In the middle of my constituency is the old church of St Margaret's. It a beautiful place that is home to the memorials of William Hutton, the first historian of Birmingham; some beautiful Edward Burne-Jones windows; and, appropriately enough, a fabulous azure-blue stained-glass window depicting Abraham, the spiritual father of Judaism, Christianity and Islam. It was here that I asked a group of local faith leaders – imams, priests, vicars, convenors and preachers – to come together to talk about how we were going to use faith, not to divide our community but to bring it together. First, I wanted to understand how they saw the basic challenge of radicalisation. The key insight came from a self-confessed radical Catholic priest, not long back from several years' work in Africa.

'What is so wrong about anger?' he said. 'Surely anger is a good thing. After all, Jesus was a radical. Muhammad was a radical. If we had no anger in society – anger at injustice or the state of the status quo – then we would never have any social progress.'

This is when it struck me. Anger is a good thing. Anger is the source of social progress. The conveyor belt theory is wrong because the journey towards violence is more like 'the fork in the road'.

For many different reasons, people get angry about 'the West'. Some then reach a fork in the road. One fork leads to acting on anger through peaceful means: voting, campaigning, founding the Stop the War coalition or standing to be the Leader of the Labour Party. Most people take this fork. A tiny minority, however, take the other fork: the path that leads to violence. And the problem with extremists today is that they tend to use religion – either

ISIS-style heresy, or 'DIY-Islam' – to persuade people to settle those grievances not by voting but through violence, motivating young people to seek, in the words of Louise Richardson, the vice chancellor of Oxford University, 'renown, revenge, and reaction'.[65]

The tractor beam at this great junction of moral choice, bending people towards violence, is, very often, not God but grievance. In and of itself, anger at injustice is not a bad thing. Little change in life is driven by those who are content with the status quo. The question we confront is, how do we channel people towards creating change through the ballot box rather than the bomb?

If we want people to take good paths to progress and not bad ones, we need a new strategy. We need to create a country where people are far more likely to seek democratic, non-violent change in the society around them, a country where they actually

---

65 See Louise Richardson, *What Terrorists Want: Understanding the Terrorist Threat* (John Murray, 2006).

feel part of our shared past and shared future, where people are equipped with a strong moral compass that helps them tell right from wrong and, crucially, where people can see realistic options – and indeed examples – to effect change, through civil society, through public service, and indeed through democratic action.

CHAPTER 5

THE HOME WE BUILD TOGETHER

Britain's first Muslim Cabinet minister, Baroness Sayeeda Warsi, has an insightful phrase: 'It's human instinct to want to matter and to want to belong … when you don't feel you either matter or belong, you're much more vulnerable to joining the extremists.'

If we want to create a society in which we destroy the idea that there is some kind of a great 'clash of civilisations' and where angry, passionate people choose peaceful paths of change, we will have to do much more to create a sense that Britain is a shared home for all.

Britain has always been a diverse place: we are English, Scottish, Welsh and Northern Irish. Towns and cities have their own sense of identity, and people of different faiths and of none have long found Britain an inclusive and tolerant country. We think it entirely natural to be of Irish heritage and proud of it, as well as being a Londoner and British. We respect people's right to identify with the gay community and where they live and their religion and their football team. We recognise, as Linda Colley of Princeton University put it:

> Identities are not like hats. Human beings can and do put on several at a time. Great Britain did not emerge by way of 'blending' of the different regional or older national cultures contained within its boundaries as is sometimes maintained … instead Britishness was superimposed over an array of internal differences.

Unlike France, we've never sought to evangelise a 'civic religion'. We've never found identity a zero–sum game. You do not have to be less of a Christian, or less of a Sikh, to be more of a British citizen.[66]

Our tolerance and liberalism have never been unconditional, however. Our diversity has always been underwritten by a subscription to a common set of values – commitment to Britain and its people, loyalty to our legal and political institutions, fairness and open-mindedness, freedom of speech, respect for others, responsibility towards others and a tradition of tolerance. And these values do mark us out – in Europe at least. Twenty-eight per cent of British citizens say 'the rule of law' is most important to them personally; the EU average is just 17 per cent.

But our 'shared values' have been under pressure for years. Once upon a time, perhaps we didn't need to state just what it meant to be British. But since the

---

66   See L. Byrne and R. Kelly, *A Common Place* (Fabian Society, 2007), http://www.fabians.org.uk/publications/a-common-place/

'50s and '60s, the 'ties that bind us' have become an awful lot weaker. The proportion of people generally trusting others has fallen from around 60 per cent in 1959 to 30 per cent in 2005.[67] As it happens, it's not just us experiencing this problem.

Robert Putnam is one of the leading thinkers on this issue. He points out that, as the Second World War generation dies out, 'a generation with a trust quotient of nearly 80 per cent was being rapidly replaced by one with a trust quotient of barely half that'. He pinpoints *eleven* different things that weaken connections between us[68] and thereby deplete social trust – from busyness and time pressure, movement of women into the labour force, residential mobility, suburbanisation, TV, changes to marriage and the welfare state, to the arrival of the '60s, bringing with it Vietnam, Watergate and the cultural revolution against authority.

---

67   'How Integrated is Modern Britain?', Social Integration Commission, p. 22.

68   Putnam, *Bowling Alone* (Simon & Schuster, 2000), p. 141.

So, how do we put things back together again? How do we create a country where we're all sort of on the same page? Over the past decade in inner-city Birmingham, I've had to think about this a lot. And so, here's my list of top reforms that I've become convinced could make a difference.

1. BRITISH VALUES OR SHARED IDEALS?

Surely it has to start with a conversation about the things we have in common.

I've been asking people for years just what it is they love about our country. What I tend to hear is a brilliant list of old favourites. The BBC. Beer in a decent British pub. Fashion and fish and chips. Our stunning countryside, chocolate, cider, our seasons and our sense of humour. The great English language. Family, friends, friendliness and football. Law and order, common sense, community spirit. The Royals and rugby. Good manners, queueing and a nice cup of tea. All the things you'd miss if you were scooped up and plonked on a desert island to talk musical favourites with that nice Kirsty Young.

Nearly ten years ago, I was rewriting British citizenship laws. To get me going, I tripped round the country asking people what are the 'rules' of being British? And crucially, what do we expect people to sign up to, if they want to join the club?

The answers were fascinating. I found we are not a nation of Alf Garnetts. We are a nation that is comfortable with difference. It's why we love a good eccentric, and I suspect it comes, in part, from the persistent strength of Britain's local identities. Time and again, when I asked how we should celebrate Britain, people pointed to a celebration of what they liked locally – whether it was something reminiscent of Trafalgar Day (mentioned in Portsmouth) or the St Paul's Carnival (mentioned in Bristol).

What annoys us is when we sense officialdom 'bending over backwards' to 'avoid giving offence' – at the expense of these old traditions (such as nativity plays being banned because they might be divisive).

This was seen as 'political correctness gone mad'. In a largely secular society, we do have only a rather vague sense of what shared British standards look like – until we bump into something hard-edged that seems like a direct challenge to norms such as 'tolerance' and 'freedom of speech'. So, Brits generally feel that anyone from different backgrounds can have different cultural traditions and religious practices, but they worry that cultural differences – for instance language, religious dress and the natural propensity to live together – get in the way of integration.

What's most striking is that people in Britain think the deal to becoming British is actually pretty simple. First, in a debate without too many absolutely fixed points, learning English is absolutely one of them. Second, people do think tolerance is vital. As one chap in Croydon put it to me: 'Being British is about accepting other cultures' and the quid pro quo was that people should be free to have their own cultural identity, and that often British citizens needed to understand different cultures and religions better, too.

But a basic point that many wanted to emphasise was summed up well by one participant in Bristol: 'It's important to make clear to newcomers that laws in this country don't come from the Church – [it] can be seen as racial prejudice to insist on this, but it's so important.' Third comes 'working hard and paying taxes'. And fourth comes 'obeying the law', by which we mean 'Parliament's law'.

So it's not complicated. Speak English. Be tolerant of other people. Work hard and pay tax. And obey the law.

Now, politicians have obsessed about 'shared values' for at least the past decade. And lo and behold, we do now have an 'official list' of British values. Can you guess what's on it? You would be forgiven for getting it wrong. It's a slightly random list, which has the big essentials such as democracy, the rule of law, individual liberty, separation of the judiciary and the executive, and mutual respect and tolerance of those with different faiths and beliefs. But in a very British way, it's not written up on big signs in government buildings, at the border, or in our schools. No – it's buried away deep in the government's 2011 Prevent strategy.

This is ludicrous. From Magna Carta to the Glorious Revolution to the European Convention on Human Rights, the natives of these islands have helped shape the rules of civilised behaviour for over eight centuries. Yet the values we hold dear are buried away in a bureaucratic policy document. This isn't good enough. In the years ahead, we should change this – and soon we'll have a chance to do so.

The government is shortly to disinter and breathe new life into an idea of Gordon Brown's – for a new British Bill of Rights. I think it's a good idea. But what it needs is a magnificent preamble that actually sets out the rights *and* responsibilities we think make for a good society. And my work tells me we need a slightly longer list of British values than the government proposes.

I serve the biggest Muslim constituency in Britain, so I was fascinated to see just how my constituents' views on British values reflect the wider national picture. Guess what? They are exactly the same. In multicultural Birmingham, people hold dear the same values as the rest of the country: freedom, equality, diversity, tolerance and respect. Brummies love our city's people, history, diversity and sense of community spirit. They believe that what makes Birmingham great is that people work twice as hard because of the challenges the city faces.

All of my research tells me that if there is one more idea that needs to go on the official list of British values, it's good old-fashioned British compassion. In fact, in every survey I've ever done on 'British' values, kindness, compassion and 'looking after the needy' – and indeed one another – are qualities that people think make our country special. This is why in poll after poll on our favourite institutions, up there with the Queen and our magnificent armed forces, is the amazing NHS: it is compassion in action.

So why don't we add 'compassion' to the official list of British values? I think there would two distinct advantages to doing so.

First, it would honour the role of faith in our national life. For many, faith is the source of the compassion they put to work making our country an amazing place to live. As one of my constituents put it to me, 'Respect for one another, kindness, helping our neighbours, working to do good in our community – these are human values that are British and Christian and Islamic.'

Second, compassion is one of the ways in which we can bring people together in civil society, volunteering and charity work. As the former Chief Rabbi Jonathan Sacks once put it, compassion teaches us how 'to build a home together'. What better lesson could we teach our children – never mind each other?

And there's one more big change I would make. A problem with 'values' is that they often smack of the past. They feel like they're handed to you, in a take-it-or-leave-it sort of way. They risk being as inspiring as a dusty heirloom. The challenge of teaching 'British values' was bluntly brought home to me by one local headteacher, who told me, 'Frankly, kids feel less British if it feels like we're forcing British values down their throat.' They feel it is something 'done to them' rather than something they shape.

Giving young people a sense that they too are co-authors of the future is important if we want to crack what many young people in new communities struggle with. So, I think it would be far more inspirational if we presented our ideas not as values – but as *ideals*. Ideals we want to live up to. Ideals that inspire our future. Ideals that might help create a climate where young people feel we live in a country where they can thrive – and contribute.

Just out of interest, I spent a few months visiting all the secondary schools in my patch to ask young people what sort of ideals inspire them. The teenagers I've spoken to want to have the debate. They're acutely aware that young people, as one teenager put it to me, 'are much easier to brainwash'; 'Young kids are influenced by what they see,' said another.

Ask a bunch of teenagers in inner-city Birmingham what they love about their country and their

WHICH FOUR OR FIVE OF THE FOLLOWING VALUES, IF ANY, WOULD YOU SAY ARE THE MOST IMPORTANT FOR LIVING IN BRITAIN?

Values	Respondents (per cent)
Respect for the law	64
Tolerance and politeness towards others	54
Freedom of speech and expression	42
Respect for all faiths	34
Justice and fair play	33

Source: Ipsos MORI.

community, and you get a fascinating response. There's something rather inspiring about adolescents extolling the importance of 'tolerance and patience', courtesy, freedom, humanity, equality, empathy, respect, democracy, diversity and the rule of law.

But a couple of ideals are absolutely key. First is the idea of mutual respect, freedom of speech and tolerance, which means 'we don't fear each other' and which creates a climate that allows people 'to be what they want to be', and 'to be the best they can be'.

The second is the recurring theme of achievement and aspiration. 'Here [in Britain] we have lots of opportunities to become whatever we want,' said one young man, while a young woman told me, 'Everyone has the same opportunity – it doesn't matter what background you come from … You're free here to get your education and pursue your dreams. You don't get that in other countries.' Ask them what they would miss if they were dumped on a desert island, and they say, 'I'd miss the chances that Britain gives.'

This should be a big national debate. We need to have the confidence to look to the kind of future we want to build together – and not simply to a past, dim, distant and behind us.

2. MAKING SENSE OF THE PAST

The past, however, offers an important opportunity, especially the business of giving young people a sharper sense of their history in general and how their ancestors helped build the Britain of today in particular. Because for millions of immigrants in Britain, unbeknown to them, the blood of their ancestors is mixed into our foundations.

Exploring the 'identity challenge' in workshops with parents, I've been struck how one theme that comes back time and time again is the challenge of an 'identity crisis'. Many parents in my constituency have either immigrated to Britain themselves, or are second-generation immigrants. They worry that their kids are prone to crises of identity. As one young mum put it to me, 'Our kids are losing their home identity. They don't know who they are. They ask themselves whether they really fit in – and it causes them to question or to look for another identity to escape to. Young people don't question their identity until people question them.'

Sitting in a slightly cold, brightly lit community hall in Birmingham's Hall Green, I spent an evening hearing about one radical way of changing this. On the table as I walked in were some unusual artefacts.

A Lee–Enfield rifle. A bullet-pierced shovel. An old
bayonet. The battered helmet of a First World War
soldier. And standing before a projector screen were
two slightly awkward-looking young men, about
to explain the project that had just fundamentally
changed 'who they thought they were'.

Listening to them, I rapidly became convinced
that British Future's experimental project,[69] teaching children how to explore the contribution of
400,000 Muslim soldiers to the First World War,
has the potential to help thousands of young Brits
see how their past is deeply entwined with the nation
they call home, revealing the rich legacy of Muslim
participation in British life.

The project, which has been developed in three
British cities, along with cadets and staff at the
Royal Military Academy Sandhurst, asks mixed
teams to investigate stories, interview Birmingham

---

69   The project is a collaboration between think-tank British Future
     and the organisation New Horizons for British Islam.

descendants of Indian Muslims who fought in the Great War, trace personal roots and present the results.

Listening to youngsters from youth clubs in Lozells and Kingstanding, I was captivated. Here were young people learning for the first time about how their great-great-grandparents or great-great-uncles left their villages and signed up in centres such as Rawalpindi and Jhelum.

Most had, hitherto, not known that Muslims had contributed to the war, or heard of men such as Sepoy Khudadad Khan of the 129th Baluchis Regiment, who was the sole survivor of a team assigned to defend British ports. He held out until reinforcements arrived, and became the first man of colour to win the Victoria Cross. Some of the 100,000 Muslims who died were buried in one of the biggest graves of the war in Mesopotamia. Most saw action in regiments such as the 30th Punjab, the 19th Lancers or the 106 Hazara Pioneers.

These young people learned about the damage a

bullet does. They heard for the first time how their ancestors 'faced the same enemy keeping these Isles safe'. One young man said to me, 'If more was known it'd help create a more cohesive society', while another said, 'This has literally changed the way I walk down the street.' Surprise, surprise – all the young Muslim participants felt 'more British' by the end of it. Yet, today, only one in five Britons know that Muslims fought for the UK. Only 2 per cent can correctly estimate the contribution offered by 1.5 million Indian soldiers, of whom 400,000 were Muslim.

These new approaches to history in general, and Remembrance in particular, have huge potential to shape a different story about the home we share today. Last year, an estimated one million Muslims wore remembrance poppies, and the 'poppy hijab', commemorating the first Muslim soldier to be awarded a VC, hit the headlines. What's more, these new ideas would be popular; 80 per cent of us say it's important for our integration for children to be aware of shared histories.

3. POWER TO THE PEOPLE

There is an important corollary to giving people a better sense of their stake in the nation's past, and that's giving people a sense that they are part of its future; that they can influence the direction we take as a country – by helping to run it.

The United Kingdom has mastered this challenge many times over the past three hundred years. Indeed, we learned the art very early in our history. Jacobean invasion forces crossed the border from the north and headed south three times after the act of Union between England and Scotland. In 1745, Bonnie Prince Charlie made it as far as Derby. That occasion was the trigger for the bloodbath of rebel forces at Culloden and the forced clearances of the Highlands that followed.

What has fascinated me for years is what happened next. One of the best historians of the period is Professor Linda Colley. In her seminal book, *Britons*, Professor Colley describes how, after the fighting finished, a grey Conservative politician, Henry Pelham, presided over one of the first and most extraordinary acts of integration in British politics, as leading Scots were systematically woven into the new power structure of the United Kingdom. When we met at the House of Commons, Professor Colley explained that, for many, there was a clear economic rationale for union – that trade could flow freely across the borders. But after Culloden, there was a strong sense, that '[t]hey [the Scots] must have their quota of patronage'.[70]

As the power of Scotland's Highland chieftains was systematically destroyed,[71] the new United Kingdom made a decisive effort to recruit Scots into Royal Service; 'I am all for having always in our army as many Scottish soldiers as possible,' said

---

70 Professor Linda Colley, private interview.

71 See Linda Colley, *Britons: Forging the Nation 1707–1837* (Yale University Press, 1992).

the Secretary of War Lord Barrington to Parliament in 1751.[72] By the mid-eighteenth century, one in four regimental officers – and a quarter of the East India Company's army officers – were Scottish[73] and some were reaching the very top of their profession.[74] By 1780, half of Scotland's MPs were employed in some kind of state office (compared to just eight in 1747). In the decade after 1775, Scots made up nearly half of the 249 'writers' appointed in Bengal, and 60 per cent of the 371 free merchants. Indeed, the de facto Governor General of India, Warren Hastings, was so surrounded by Scots, they were known as his 'Scotch guardians'.

Today, Birmingham is one of the most diverse cities in the world – certainly one of the most diverse

---

72 Colley, ibid., p.125.

73 Colley, ibid., p.132.

74 John Campbell, 4th Earl of Loudoun, wound up as Commander in Chief of British forces in North America during the Seven Years' War. Hector Munro became Britain's first Governor of Canada in 1760.

cities in the United Kingdom. The city is well on course to become the first 'ethnic minority-majority' city in Britain. Yet one of the things you notice working in Birmingham politics is how white the power structure remains. Have we learned the lesson from the United Kingdom's creation? I asked ministers if they would assess the levels of representation from the black and minority ethnic communities in the governance of our local spending bodies. I think it's fair to say ministers told me to get lost. Politely, the Minister for Women and Equalities said she had 'no plans for [such] an assessment'.[75] So I did one myself.

I tabled freedom of information requests to the fifty-eight organisations in the city that spend public money, and asked them for the ethnic minority breakdown of their top ten leaders. Four organisations said they did not know, including, oddly

---

75 http://www.theyworkforyou.com/wrans/?id=2015-07-08.6111.h&s=speaker per cent3A11360#g6111.q0

enough, the West Midlands Police. In total, however, I was given information on 561 leaders across the public sector. Now, in Birmingham, the 'white British' population makes up 52 per cent of the population. Yet nearly 80 per cent of our 561 leaders are 'white British'. Eighteen organisations including two universities, hospitals and the fire service had no leaders from an ethnic minority among their top ten leaders.

Simple studies like this are fraught with problems, but this study does highlight an issue. When we have nearly a third of public spending bodies with no one from an ethnic minority at the top table, in one of Britain's most diverse cities, then we have work to do to ensure the power structure of the city reflects the community that calls it home.

4. THE MORAL COMPASS

If our young people get angry with the state of society, we want them to reach the junction or the fork in the road and make the right choice. We want them to choose a path that is peaceful, not violent. When they arrive at the fork in the road, we want our children to have the best possible moral compass. And that means we need to change the way we teach them.

Most of today's education is about the world *around* our children. We do not really think to cultivate children's understanding of what's inside them: their personalities, their characters, the people they could be. Think about what most parents want for their children. No doubt we all want them to have a sense of Britain's *values*, but more important still is a sense of *virtue*; a sense of what is right and what is wrong. Last year, half of referrals to de-radicalisation programmes came from schools.

Professor James Arthur is the pro-vice chancellor of Birmingham University, and as head of the school of education he led an extraordinary programme of research in Hodge Hill's schools exploring aspirations, ethics – and character. The point

Professor Arthur makes about character education is simple:

> Character education is about the acquisition and strengthening of virtues: the traits that sustain a well-rounded life and a thriving society. That means virtues like courage, justice, honesty, compassion for others, self-discipline, gratitude, humility and modesty. This isn't about 'indoctrination' or mindless conditioning. The ultimate goal of all proper character education is to equip students with the intellectual tools to make wise choices.

If we're to maximise the chances of our young people succeeding, avoiding danger and getting a job, we need to teach them the skills and aptitudes that business needs. Six in ten firms say school and college leavers have not developed the self-management skills they need for work.

This is why 'character education' is so important.

We have to acknowledge that for our young people, real power is not only the hard stuff of exams; it's the harder stuff of how the world works. What we once called 'soft skills' are, for many in the inner city, the most important skills of all.

Studying several thousand children in Hodge Hill over the course of two years, Professor Arthur's team found young people were generally optimistic about their futures.[76] They had no collective sense that they might be held back by their location. Parents were also ambitious and optimistic about their children's futures. But here was the challenge: Hodge Hill is a typical inner-city community. It boasts the highest youth unemployment in Britain. It is surrounded by motorways and big trunk roads, and at times we can feel like an island. There is no strong, all-inclusive sense of community; population mobility is high, and there are few amenities.

---

76 http://www.learningforlife.org.uk/wplife/wp-content/uploads/2010/06/Citizens-of-Character_SUMMARY.pdf

Crucially, Professor Arthur found that:

> The local community provides very few public
> amenities to stimulate the development of char-
> acter skills, with few public libraries, community
> centres, youth clubs or sporting facilities acces-
> sible to young people. *This means that there are few*
> *places available for the cultivation of a common citizen-*
> *ship or a sense of shared life. Opportunities to exercise civic*
> *and social virtues such as leadership, volunteering, cour-*
> *age, charity, toleration and respect are extremely limited.*
> [My italics]

This is why character education in our schools is so
important: quite simply, there are not a lot of other
places for it to happen. The problem for Britain is
that character education is not compulsory in every
school. Indeed, every school has the freedom to either
pursue this agenda – or to ignore it. One study found
that schools which offer character education tend to
have a 'key teacher' who goes that extra mile. Very few

teachers receive special training, and most believe school assessment frameworks hinder their efforts.[77]

Worse, the legal duty on academies, free and independent schools to teach balanced religious or character education is weak. New regulations published in 2014 mean schools must actively promote British values of democracy, rule of law, individual liberty and mutual respect and tolerance of those with different faiths and beliefs, and offer spiritual, moral, social and cultural development. But they are not required to teach citizenship skills at eleven to fourteen, or fourteen to sixteen. As we discovered during the so-called Trojan Horse affair in Birmingham schools, it was much too easy for academies to opt out of agreed local protocols designed to deliver a balanced religious education.[78] Given the chal-

---

77   J. Arthur et al., 'Character Education in UK Schools', Birmingham University.

78   Schools were freed of local accountability without any form of alternative oversight. As such, they opted out of the local religious education framework, known as SACRE, yet the Secretary of State made no determination or enquiries about

lenges we face as a country, I'm not sure that is wise. There obviously should be training for teachers; each school should have a lead expert, and all should have a character education policy with extra-curricular activities to encourage character development.

5. UNIVERSAL COMMUNITY SERVICE

An important complement to 'character education' has to be universal community service. If we want to cultivate a sense among young people that they are not outsiders, but insiders with a role to play in making society better and with the power to make a difference, then it is vital that we work hard connecting them to the world around them.

Many young people in our inner cities feel no such connection. They feel adrift. And so they turn

arrangements for collective worship and religious education. See James Arthur, 'Extremism and Neo-Liberal Education Policy: A Contextual Critique of the Trojan Horse Affair in Birmingham Schools', *British Journal of Educational Studies*, No. 63/3, 2015.

to closed, tight communities for a sense of belong-
ing. Communities called gangs. From here, it is too
often a short step to violence. Birmingham is a city
that used to have a lot of experience of the problem.

One of the frontline pioneers tackling the city's
challenge was Commander Tom Coughlan, one of
the most inspiring public servants I have ever met,
and leader of Birmingham's Tackling Gangs Partner-
ship. Headquartered on an industrial estate behind
some anonymous doors, he explained to me the root
cause of the gang activity he was tackling:

> It springs from a lack of capable guardianship at
> a young age – however you choose to define it –
> moral, spiritual, physical or emotional. It's then
> compounded by poor educational attainment and
> an attitude in some schools that they would be
> better off out [of] the school. Then you get early
> offending or disruptive behaviour.
>
> But many of the young people in gangs start
> off by presenting a vulnerability. They might be a

victim of crime and then join a gang for the sense of protection. Then they're required to offend to develop status. Then they might be a victim once again and before long they're confronted with action with only two outcomes. Either they go to prison. Or death.

One of the young probation officers working for the team told me a story that has stayed with me: the story of an offender they had been helping to build a new life. His mother was so worried about the young man getting mixed up again with the old problems he faced before prison, she actually bought him a house in a different place – only for the local council to refuse to let him into their patch. Not long after, he was stabbed to death. At a memorial service organised by his family, his mother said this: 'How is it that his parents' generation could go from Jamaica to Birmingham, to build a new life, when today some of our young people will not even go from Aston to Handsworth?'

Community service isn't cheap, but it's perhaps one of the most important investments we can make. Back in 2008, Prime Minister Gordon Brown set a goal that every young person should undertake at least fifty hours of community service in their teenage years. Today, the government runs a programme, The Challenge, that gives some young people fourteen days' community service over a summer holiday, followed by four social action days. The effect is amazing; by the end of the programme, The Challenge found 72 per cent of young people agreed with the statement 'I am more able to trust people'.[79]

6. FROM 'PREVENT' TO 'SAFEGUARD'

Despite our best efforts, we have to accept that sometimes, things will go wrong. Sometimes, as children

---

79 Research published by NCS provider, The Challenge. See http://the-challenge.org/component/content/article/32-questions-parents/143-who-can-do-the-challenge

grow up they will be seduced by malign influences. Teenagers, by their very nature, are explorers. Sometimes, they end up in dark places.

There will therefore always be a need for public servants who work on the frontline with children to be on the lookout for those in trouble – and these professionals will sometimes need back-up, to bring a child back from the brink and to a place of safety.

Aware of this, the UK government introduced what is known as the Prevent duty on public authorities to identify children they deem at risk of radicalisation. This is not easy stuff. Indeed, we are struggling with it all over the West. Federico Ragazzi is a professor at the University of Leiden and one of the authors of a European Parliament report on tackling radicalisation. He makes a simple point: there is no clear 'firewall' between social integration work and police work, and this creates huge problem in building the requisite levels of trust required to engage young people in a journey back to safety.

Countries all over Europe are wrestling with the issue.[80]

France has created a network of public de-radicalisation centres.

The Belgian government created a Federal Programme for Preventing Violent Radicalisation, and in Verviers is testing a prevention unit composed of radicalisation experts, psychologists and social workers.

The Norwegians created, in 2014, a programme for Action Against Radicalisation and Violent Extremism, with a sharp focus on combating radicalisation through the internet.

The Danish strategy on combating radicalisation dates back to 2009, with a programme that puts a strong emphasis on direct work with vulnerable young people.

The challenge is, as one senior police officer put it to me, that 'this is very similar to a gangs issue.

---

80 These case studies highlighted in Council of Europe report, op. cit.

And what you find dealing with gangs, is that you can never arrest your way out of the problem.' Some kind of social work will always be needed, but the police need to be part of the equation for two simple reasons.

First, to make an assessment of whether someone is at risk, you need to build a jigsaw puzzle. Some professionals, such as teachers, might have some pieces of the puzzle, like news, innocently reported, that a family is planning a nice summer holiday in Syria. But second, the other pieces of the puzzle might be held by the police, and might have been acquired using legal, but covert means.

Someone, somewhere has to put the pieces of the puzzle together to draw a judgement about whether a child is at risk. And some children are at risk. For instance, in October 2015 newspapers reported that a *baby* was among more than twenty children made subject to court orders. James Munby, the President of the Family Division of the High Court, referred to six cases involving allegations that children, with their parents, 'are planning or being groomed to travel to parts of Syria controlled by the so-called Islamic State'.

Second, where a young person is in contact with a radicaliser, the radicaliser may well be committing a criminal offence. And so they might need arresting.

There is no simple strategy to getting this right, but what is now clear is that the Prevent 'brand' in Britain has become so distrusted, for good reasons and bad, that a new approach is needed. The simplest is to bring the focus back to the purpose of the exercise, which is keeping the child safe. The 'prevent' duty, therefore, needs to be recast as a simple safeguarding duty and coupled with the broader legal obligations of frontline staff to keep young people safe – and to share information between themselves where they think a child is at risk. Just as schools have Special Educational Needs Coordinators or SENCOs[81] to provide focused help for children with

---

81   Experts in special educational needs.

special needs, so every school in Britain now needs a 'PREVENTCO', a safeguarding leader trained to keep children safe from the malign influences of extremism.

CONCLUSION

Finally, we need to rediscover our enthusiasm for a shared celebration of what we have in common. For many years, I thought this might be best achieved with a new Britain Day[82] – a moment in the calendar when we celebrate what we love about the United Kingdom, modelled on the successful example of Australia's annual Australia Day. But the truth is, this does not make sense in a country where, at the last census, 70 per cent identified themselves as English – and only 29 per cent as British. As Lord Ashcroft Polls discovered, support for UKIP draws on an inchoate sense of identity under pressure;

---

82   See, for instance, L. Byrne, *A More United Kingdom* (Demos, 2008).

as one focus group reported, 'You can't fly a St George's flag anymore; you can't call Christmas Christmas; you can't wear an England shirt in the bus … you can't speak up about these things because you'll be called a racist.'

Dissolving this sense of grievance is an important step towards a more united country. 'Englishness' is today a stronger national identity everywhere other than London, and generally people agree with the idea that 'paying more attention to Englishness will help us unite communities and bring us all together.'[83] Two-thirds of people now feel St Patrick's Day is more widely celebrated than St George's Day. Three-quarters want St George's Day celebrated more and 41 per cent say the lack of a day off is the reason we don't celebrate. So let's fly the flag of St George, make 'Jerusalem' the English anthem, and make St George's Day a bank holiday. We should be prepared to party in pursuit of progress.

---

83   See Katwala et al., *Making Citizenship Matter* (British Future, 2016).

CHAPTER 6

THE DIGITAL DANGER SLIDE

The shocking case of Boy S, the fifteen-year-old Blackburn teenager convicted of inciting terrorism, revealed a new truth in the battle against extremism.[84] In shocking testimony, the police laid bare the crucial role of social media through which Boy S was first groomed, and through which he planned mayhem.

---

84 See, among other coverage, 'Britain's Youngest Jihadi Must Never Be Named', *Daily Mail*, 3 October 2015; 'Teenage Terrorist Gets Life, But He Cannot Be Named', *Daily Telegraph*, 3 October 2015.

In a Manchester courtroom, the most appalling story unfolded. Prosecutors revealed the boy, radicalised at fourteen and bullied at school, had threatened teachers and classmates with beheading. He acquired a smartphone, built himself a fantasy digital image and became a minor celebrity in online jihadi circles, with 24,000 Twitter followers. When his content became too disturbing, Twitter closed his accounts. But he just kept opening new ones: eighty-nine of them in all.

He was arrested after he connected with an eighteen-year-old Australian, Sevdet Besim, through an expert ISIS recruiter based in the Middle East. The recruiter helped Boy S talk through a plot to behead a police officer at an Anzac parade on the other side of the world in Melbourne. Boy S and his henchman exchanged an incredible 3,000 encrypted messages and when he was arrested Boy S was discovered to be researching bomb-making for a list of targets that included a police station, a town hall and BAE Systems. He kept a combat knife and ISIS flag in his bedroom, and a martyrdom video on his phone.

The boy's teenage girlfriend – who also pleaded guilty – was found to have exchanged over 16,000 messages in eight days with the boy.

The case of Boy S reveals the new reality of what we now confront: the frontline is online, and it is here that we confront a new digital danger slide, like a roller-coaster, capable of taking a young person from rage to radicalisation and from radicalisation to battle-readiness in the space of weeks.

The government might introduce whatever constraints it likes on free speech; it might try to take a 'tougher line' on mosques, but the idea risks backfiring badly when the problem is not radical preachers in backrooms – but in chatrooms.

ENRAGED

If you are a young British Muslim and you're feeling, like any teenager, a bit unsure about your identity, then today's media environment is a disaster zone. There are few places better designed to make you feel more alone, alienated or, indeed, 'a stranger in your own land'.

My work with young people in Birmingham confirms that, like young people nationally, the majority now source their news and information about the world online – and from a bewildering range of sources: BBC News, the *Daily Mirror* website, Instagram, Twitter, Facebook, Snapchat, YouTube, even the *New York Times*. The list is endless. But in every school, the single most important news source was the Daily Mail Online, and, surprise, surprise, young people often find themselves disgusted by what they see as an Islamophobic diet of hate. 'There are always these racist posts on Islam. There's lots of disrespect there – which you just don't see for other religions.' In particular, young people notice the lack of positive Muslim role models.

Very few of these news sources carry what you might call a positive news flow about Muslims. Quite the contrary. I surveyed my constituents to ask what they thought was responsible for today's rise in Islamophobia. They were crystal clear: 82 per cent believed that the media was responsible for the rise of Islamophobia.

We face 'constant media distortion of all Muslims', said one young woman. 'Media. Media. Media,' said another, when I asked what was fuelling Islamophobia. A middle-aged man explained:

> The mainstream media continuously showing terrorism and relating it to Muslims and Islam is only bringing hatred and a negative image of this religion. Everyone that has committed a crime and has a Muslim name or even a beard and eastern looks is advertised on every mainstream media channel especially the BBC and *Daily Mail* as Muslim and you can read this in their heading and subheadings. The articles then populate the report with all previous acts of terrorism up till 9/11.

'I think news channels are responsible who only show one-sided stories,' one man in his thirties told me.

'As soon as a Muslim commits a crime they are named as Muslim, whereas whenever a crime is committed by someone else it will be called as a man or woman.'

'Media!' said another young woman.

The media portray a very extreme and false image of the religion. Whenever a Muslim commits a mistake the religion is tarnished and suffers the outcome of the individual. When a non-Muslim commits a mistake, the media never mention or accuse the religion of the individual. This is blatant discrimination.

These views are reflected in the evidence I heard from young people about how they saw the media – and in particular, social media. 'The media doesn't highlight the good things,' said one teenager. 'It just highlights the bad.' 'Muslims have been othered,' said another. 'I feel we've been side-lined. I feel we're always on the back foot explaining ourselves.'

'The media is a threat to good values' was another typical comment. 'It just represents Islam in a bad way … It just misleads people about Islam and leads them to think about violence.'

In particular, young people notice it when people post derogatory comments, and notice how it causes a 'chain reaction'. It is therefore not hard to see how young Muslims can begin to question whether their country is a place they can call home.

RADICALISED

The challenge of today's digital media environment is that it now enables someone to go from enraged to radicalised in a frighteningly short space of time.

A typical experience was described for me, by Sulaimaan, the Channel mentor I met in Hodge Hill:

> [Online] they [young people] are looking for new heroes and new role models. Some people will

often go online because they want to hear from Mr Big about some big conspiracy theory. And what they find is a parallel interpretation of the world. They're listening to scholars who have risen without trace and suddenly they have got an interpretation of everything. This is like their Rosetta Stone, what a lot call their 'true tube'.

Analysis of ISIS recruitment files leaked to Sky News reveals just how dangerous some of these Mr Bigs can be. Analysis of the files by RUSI (Royal United Services Institute) found that many UK foreign fighters declared as their sponsor Omar Bakri Mohammed, the Syrian preacher who founded the group Al-Muhajiroun in the UK in the late 1990s (proscribed in 2010). Once dismissed as a 'loud-mouth', and christened by Jon Ronson as 'the Tottenham Ayatollah', he reached new recruits via the internet.

It's a change in tactics signalled in a little-discussed manual written by al Qaeda in Iraq – the group that became ISIS. 'A Course in the Art of

Recruiting' was recovered by US forces in 2009 and sets out step by step the methods deployed by ISIS groomers on instant messenger apps such as WhatsApp, Twitter, Snapchat, Instagram, Kik, Viber and a host of apps few parents have ever heard of.

The recruitment methods were clever.[85] Contact with wannabe recruits was first tested with a few toes in the water; recruiters monitored online communities that might harbour some sympathetic surfers, for example, by watching accounts that followed CAGE, an advocacy group founded by Guantanamo detainee Moazzam Begg.

Once first contact is made with a target, a micro-community is formed around them with high-volume bursts of up to 250 messages a day. At this stage, recruiters become full-on, encouraging their subject to isolate themselves from the people around them, with exhortations, for example, not

---

85 See J. M. Berger, 'Tailored Online Interventions: The Islamic State's Recruitment Strategy', CTC Sentinel, October 2015.

to befriend non-believers. Once a firm relationship is established, the subject is like a fish on a hook, and the recruiter switches to private communication, 'going dark' and taking the interaction to secure messaging services such as WhatsApp, Kik and Telegram.

One of the best descriptions of the process was given to me by a teacher with a background in safeguarding, at one of my local schools. The extraordinary *New York Times* feature 'ISIS and the Lonely Young American'[86] masterfully describes the experience of Alex, a young, isolated 23-year-old Sunday-school teacher, socially awkward, without many friends, and living with her grandparents in deep rural America. 'It gets lonely here,' she told the paper. Over the course of several months, a new set of online friends – from Manchester – emerged, talked Alex through conversion to Islam and a

86 Rukmini Callimachi, 'ISIS and the Lonely Young American', *New York Times*, 27 June 2015.

separation from her family, before finally seeking to encourage her to leave for 'a Muslim land'.

As my teacher friend explained to me, the story illustrates the 'power of the ping'. That adrenalin-fuelled moment for a young person when their social media account glows with a friendship that seems so elusive in the real world around them. Emotionally vulnerable, they become far easier to manipulate – as every groomer knows.

There is now more and more evidence of the huge role played by social media in the radicalisation process. The RAND group recently published a survey remarkable for the sheer diversity of case studies,[87] including a British male, born in Pakistan, who came to the UK when young and began using the internet to access bomb-making websites. He met his wife on the internet, and she too accessed bomb-making websites and downloaded

---

87 See http://www.rand.org/content/dam/rand/pubs/research_reports/RR400/RR453/RAND_RR453.pdf

beheading videos, regularly searching for public armed forces events. Another was a male who converted to Islam at a Birmingham mosque on the first anniversary of 7/7. Online, he searched violent extremist propaganda and instructions on how to build suicide vests and explosives. Another, a London teenager, used the internet to socialise with members of the now-proscribed group Al-Muhajiroun. Another joined friends in creating a 'resistance group' with an online profile, claiming an al Qaeda-sponsored remit and threatening national political figures, publishing incitements to murder. A pair of brothers used digital technology to make videos of themselves using weapons. Another was identified and approached through the internet by a terrorist facilitator in Pakistan, who made regular visits to the UK, collected information on chemical weapons and began to discuss arrangements for military training in Pakistan.

The internet is not the exclusive domain of Islamic extremists, of course. A white British male from the North of England became a member of the same online right-wing group as his father and was arrested, along with his father, for offences including inciting racial violence. He used the internet to engage in online debates, contact members of the online right-wing group and develop friendships with white supremacists from across Europe.

So the internet increases opportunities for self-radicalisation but, crucially, most cases of so-called 'online self-radicalisation' involve virtual communication and interaction with others, online and more recently in encrypted messaging apps.

BATTLE READY

Today these apps are being used to pervert angry young minds with propaganda produced like pop videos, iconic images of the Knights of Lone Jihad and twisted snippets from the Quran, used to justify murder. And we're not fighting back. In my patch of East Birmingham, police, parents and teachers are worried. Once, Napoleon said an army marches on its stomach. Now, the extremist's foot-soldiers march with a smartphone. Digital technology is as important as a sharpened blade, fertiliser and buckets of peroxide.

Crucially, the internet has triggered a revolution in the attack methods of our enemies, enabling, for the first time, a DIY-terrorism with online inspiration and targeting intelligence.

In the first days of al Qaeda-inspired violence, attacks in the UK relied on Brits who had in some way or another been connected with the long struggle against the Russians in Afghanistan. Two of the earliest terrorists to have an impact, for instance, were Tariq Mahmood and Rashid Rauf, the so-called British shoe bomber, who tried to destroy a flight from Paris to Miami in December 2001, which failed only because his damp matches failed to ignite. Both were sons of jihadists who fought in Afghanistan.

The second phase of attacks unfolded after the

airline liquid bomb plot of 2006 was organised
by terrorists who had received some sort of training and direction from the Federally Administered
Tribal Areas (FATA) on the borderlands of Afghanistan and Pakistan.

As time went by, however, the terrorist methodology evolved to the point where foreign training was
rare, and where, as in the case of Lee Rigby, attacks
were organised locally.

For some time, technology has been playing
an increasingly important role. Over the course
of 2007 and 2008, police were making more and
more arrests for counter-terrorism offences, where
bad material – bomb-making manuals or sermons
inspiring hatred – were found on personal comput-
ers, pen drives, CDs or DVDs. By 2010, terrorism
was decisively moving online. In March 2011, Rajib
Karim, a software developer with British Airways,
was convicted and sentenced to a minimum of thirty
years in prison. He had been in direct contact with
Anwar al-Awlaki, who had sent him an email asking,

'Is it possible to get a package or person with a package on board a flight heading to the US?'

Three months later, in May 2010, King's College London student Roshonara Choudhry, also radicalised over the internet by the sermons of Anwar al-Awlaki, acted in a lone-wolf attack and stabbed my friend, Labour MP Stephen Timms, in his constituency surgery. It was the first al Qaeda-inspired attack on a public figure in the United Kingdom and the first conviction in the United Kingdom of a female for a violent terrorist attack.

With the emergence of ISIS, however, came a step-change in the scale and sophistication of digital operations.[88] With a huge and well-organised media operation, *Al Hayat*, came a full-spectrum propaganda operation, with everything from videos of children holding decapitated heads, to ISIS militants posing with Nutella jars demonstrating

---

88 In particular, see Charles Winter, 'Documenting the Virtual "Caliphate"', Quilliam, 2015, and J. M. Berger and Jonathan Morgan, 'The ISIS Twitter Census', Brookings, March 2015.

local comfort levels, to a sophisticated hacking operation.[89] By November 2014, Robert Hannigan, director of GCHQ, was highlighting how ISIS was using the big US communication service providers as the 'command-and-control networks of choice'.

In one three-month period, September to December 2014, experts reckon that an incredible 46,000 Twitter accounts were in use by ISIS supporters. And the figure could have been as high as 70,000,[90] with almost one in five ISIS tweeters using English as their *lingua digital*. On average, every account boasted 1,000 followers, and issued, over the course of its existence, over 2,000 tweets. The hyperactive accounts numbered perhaps 500–2,000, but together they issued millions of tweets with over five million links, including connections to a small core of highly professional groomers looking for

---

89 See Scott Gates and Sukanya Podder, 'Social Media, Recruitment Allegiance and the Islamic State', *Perspectives on Terrorism*, Volume 9, Issue 4.

90 See Berger and Morgan, op. cit.

recruits to defect to Syria, or to mount attacks on their homeland.

For ISIS, digital propaganda became key to assisting the recruitment of up to 20,000 foreign fighters,[91] who in turn are key to powering ISIS's advance. But the Virtual Caliphate's mission is not simply to recruit, it is to attack, and for months, one man at the absolute core of the business was Birmingham-born Junaid Hussain, the eldest son of a dinner lady, who went to school round the corner from me, in Kings Heath. It was Hussain who would help take the extremist's methodology beyond inspiration to live intelligence, using social media apps to provide British collaborators with precise information about potential targets.

Junaid first met British justice when he was convicted of hacking Tony Blair's personal address book in 2012. Described as 'shy and unassuming' by his defence lawyers, he promptly hot-footed it to Syria not long after he was released two years later. There,

---

91   See Gates and Podder, op. cit.

he proved potently effective, working at the heart of the United Cyber Caliphate's team, which, on 12 January 2012, hacked the US Central Military Command's Twitter and YouTube accounts, emblazoning them in digital ink with the slogan, 'I love you ISIS'.

Large-scale hacking of French websites followed the Charlie Hebdo attacks, but what was far more serious was the acquisition of targeting information that could be relayed to attackers acting on the ground in the West. In 2015, there was clear evidence that Hussain was helping direct two Texan gunmen who opened fire at a Prophet Muhammad cartoon competition in Garland. He tweeted congratulations to the two attackers just minutes after they opened fire. He was subsequently killed in a drone strike after British ministers were satisfied he was actively involved in facilitating murder in the UK. In the aftermath, it emerged that the ISIS hacking team posted hacked personal details and mobile phone numbers of the heads of the CIA, FBI and US National Security Agency, plus 54,000 Twitter usernames and passwords.[92] Digital technology now enables our enemies to shift their collaborators from radicalised to battle-ready. So, what do we do?

BEATING THE BROADCAST OF EVIL

When Hannah Arendt sat through the trial of Nazi war criminal Adolf Eichmann, she was struck by the sheer mundanity of the man who described the genocide of the Holocaust. Eichmann, she reported, was an exercise in the '*banality* of evil'. Today, ISIS is seeking to bring shock and awe to facilitate the *broadcast* of evil. And our job is to stop them.

This insidious menace is, I am afraid, the new normal. We had better get used to it. Just as we learned to accept the need to look out for strange people buying buckets of peroxide, so do we need to acknowledge

---

92 'IS "Cyber Caliphate" Takes Over 54,000 Twitter Accounts', *Mail on Sunday*, 8 November 2015.

that constant vigilance will be the price of our freedom on the digital battlefront. What is clear is that we need a battery of measures, and like all things in public policy, progress will start with money.

High up in the towers of Scotland Yard, sitting down with the Counter Terrorism Referral Unit, I got a sense of the challenge from the frontline. Founded in 2010, its mission is to remove unlawful terrorist material from the internet, in breach of some widely drawn laws that prohibit incitement or glorification of terrorist acts.[93] So far, the team has helped take down over 140,000 pieces of terrorist-related material.

The team rely on both proactively trawling the web and on referrals that come in from the public, and they've learned to forecast 'surges' of material often linked to ISIS atrocities or new editions of extremist magazines such as *Dabiq* or *Inspire*. 'Frankly,' said one officer, 'we don't mind who sources it. We just want it down.'

---

93 Specifically, Section 3 of the Terrorism Act, 2006.

The challenges, however, are more complex than you might think.

First, many of the biggest organisations hosting content – such as Twitter or Facebook – are based in the land of free speech, the United States of America. Second, when new file-sharing sites pop up, they might in fact be run by the proverbial one man and a dog in Latvia. Tracking down the owners and persuading them to do the right thing can therefore take a little bit of time.

The speed with which extremists can move between different applications is a constant challenge. At the end of 2015, for instance, when Twitter finally started shutting down ISIS-related accounts, lots of ISIS operatives shifted first to the Russian-owned VKontakte and then to Berlin-based Telegram, creating their own channel, dubbed *Nashir* or 'Distributor', which quickly amassed 4,500 subscribers.[94]

---

94 'IS Exploits Telegram Mobile App to Spread Propaganda', BBC Online, 7 October 2015.

Following the Paris attacks, Telegram acted swiftly to suspend the accounts of seventy-eight public channels used by ISIS and its supporters in twelve languages.[95] Still, by February 2016, ISIS was boasting that it operated 10,000 Facebook accounts and 5,000 Twitter profiles.[96]

What I had not quite realised is that, in the finest traditions of British policing, officers are brilliant at taking the fastest and most effective path to 'keeping the Queen's peace'. And this means that most material is taken down, not by resorting to the law but by gently pointing out to companies that bad material is almost always in breach of community standards, and it's not good for business.

'Community standards,' said one officer, 'are much, much tougher than anything written into law. A company's terms and conditions are quite simply

---

95 Baroness Shields, 'Beyond Business: The Responsibility of Global Players', 17 January 2016.

96 'ISIS Releases 25-minute Video Complaining about Facebook', *The Times*, 26 February 2016.

the most powerful tool we've got. They're far more stringent than local laws, and we have to remember that once we get formal, and head for court, it takes time.'

Telegram, for instance, changed its tolerance level for letting extremists share bad material pretty quickly after users started complaining – they could see the damage it was doing to its business model.

The special challenge that comes with extremist material is that, very often, a judgement has to be made about whether something is on the right or wrong side of the line. Unlike images of child abuse, where anything and everything is wrong, a judgement call has to made about whether an image is glorifying or inciting violence.

The point was reinforced for me by some of the team from Google, owners of YouTube, which has had to deal with this challenge for years. Google has let users flag bad content that breaches its community standards since 2008 – and, unsurprisingly, the most flagged items turn out to be

Justin Bieber videos. The challenge is in recognising the context.

For instance, should you remove the video of the shooting of the Iranian protester Neda Agha-Soltan, whose murder sparked a serious challenge to the regime in Iran?[97] Or the footage of the self-immolation of Tunisian Mohamed Bouazizi in December 2010, which helped trigger the Arab Spring, a grass-roots, pro-democracy revolt, in part organised through social media? Or what about the barbaric ISIS videos of the brutal murder of the Jordanian pilot who was burned alive in a cage – when the entire video was broadcast on US network Fox News? Or, what about the videos of extremist preacher Anwar al-Awlaki – when the subject is Islam and obesity?

The real challenge is bigger than this. As I was leaving Scotland Yard, the officers showed me a little graphic that illustrates the sheer scale of what they

97 https://www.theguardian.com/world/2009/jun/22/neda-soltani-death-iran

are now contending with. It's the picture that shows just how much is uploaded to the internet every *minute:*[98]

- 3.3 million Facebook posts
- 342,000 tweets
- 41,000 Instagram photos
- 120 hours of video to YouTube
- and 50 *billion* WhatsApp messages

Try policing that.

And that is why we have to debate how we split the burden between policing and self-policing.

Big social media companies such as Facebook and Twitter are called 'communication service providers' and today there is no positive requirement on them to report extremist content. They claim it's impossible to monitor all the stuff that

---

98 http://uk.businessinsider.com/infographic-what-happens-online-in-60-seconds-2015-5

is posted because (a) there is so much of it and (b) once they start monitoring it, and possibly editing it, their business changes, and they become de facto publishers.

In one of the most notorious dimensions of the murder of Fusilier Lee Rigby, it emerged that a social media company, believed to be Facebook closed Michael Adebowale's accounts with an automated system because they had triggered alerts that they were associated with terrorism. But they did not report the fact that the accounts included news of his intention to commit murder.

The Commons Intelligence Select Committee took a dim view of the question, insisting that when such accounts were automatically closed, companies must 'accept their responsibility' to review the accounts and pass on any word of an intention to commit a terrorist act. The government reported that the company in question had subsequently agreed to do a better job. But, isn't that a bit vague? As it happens, EU rules stop us imposing a general obligation on companies to monitor content.[99] When French ministers proposed new laws to prosecute websites hosting extremist propaganda, lobby groups were quick to accuse politicians of proposing 'pre-emptive censorship'.[100] But we *can* impose an obligation to report *illegal* activity – and that is precisely the debate now unfolding in America.

---

99 Specifically the EU Electronic Commerce Directive provides that Member States are not permitted to impose a general obligation to monitor on CSPs. However, an obligation to report illegal activity may be imposed. 'Article 15: No general obligation to monitor', reads:

1. *Member States shall not impose a general obligation on providers, when providing the services covered by Articles 12, 13 and 14 [intermediary services], to monitor the information which they transmit or store, nor a general obligation actively to seek facts or circumstances indicating illegal activity.*
2. *Member States may establish obligations for information society service providers promptly to inform the competent public authorities of alleged illegal activities undertaken or information provided by recipients of their service or obligations to communicate to the competent authorities, at their request, information enabling the identification of recipients of their service with whom they have storage agreements.*

100 'ISIS: EU Vote on Anti-Islamist Recruitment Laws Slammed as "Nonsensical Online Censorship"', IBT, 20 October 2015.

Senator Dianne Feinstein's draft law, the Requiring Reporting of Online Terrorist Activity Act, would require technology companies to report online terrorist activity to law enforcement. It would not require companies to monitor customers, but it would insist they report any information they become aware of, such as attack planning, recruitment or distribution of terrorist material. It is modelled on legislation that requires technology companies to report online child pornography when they become aware of it.[101]

The American Civil Liberties Union (ACLU) has argued on behalf of a coalition of civil liberties, human rights and trade associations to oppose the bill, because it would create strong incentives to over-report, and, indeed, tech companies argue that 'overbroad reporting to the government, [would

---

101 18 US Code § 2258A – 'Reporting requirements of electronic communication service providers and remote computing service providers' – requires that anyone engaged in providing an electronic communications service, who becomes aware of child pornography, must inform the National Center for Missing and Exploited Children.

end up] swamping law enforcement with useless information'.[102]

Furthermore, as the *Los Angeles Times* argued:

> The bill doesn't define terrorist activity, and tech workers aren't trained to identify it or the people who should be scrutinized; after all, extremists are hardly the only ones tweeting about Islamic State videos. So if a company tries to police its network, chances are that it will report far too much to avoid overlooking something important. That would only pile more hay onto the stack that investigators have to pick through, rather than helping to uncover more needles.[103]

So we know that technology companies will tell us that it's impossible for them to monitor so much

---

102 Internet Association, 5 August 2015, internetassociation.org

103 'Bill Targeting Terrorist Propaganda on the Internet Misses the Mark', *Los Angeles Times*, 9 December 2015.

content, and to pre-screen it all before it goes live. But let's remember this. Some of these firms are the most profitable on the planet. In fact, Apple is *the* most profitable firm. Making money from free speech has got to carry some obligations to free speech. And one of those obligations must be to avoid facilitating its abuse.

Of course we should be realistic. The sheer scale of the challenge that comes from a world with more smartphones than people will mean that there is never going to be a substitute for equipping our children with the ability to tell right from wrong in the digital world.

I've talked about this with parents in Birmingham. They're very, very worried. When you ask mums and dads about their concerns for their kids on the internet, they say, as one mum did, '[You do worry] they will be groomed, targeted online. Companies do not follow their own policies – and [kids] may make mistakes which put themselves at risk.' There is a widespread feeling that companies do not do enough or make sure that messages, posts and sharing meet the standards of their own policies. Crucially, parents feel that switching on safeguard controls needs to be easier – especially for new smartphones. And companies should be fined when content on their site is inappropriate.

Parents are obviously the key to keeping their children safe, and lots of the young people I've spoken to in my research relay the conversations they've had with their parents watching the news about extremists' behaviour – especially at the time when ISIS's hateful videos were first published. One young man said to me, 'We watched the news of the videos on the telly – and then my mum took me through the different bits of the Quran to show me where it says that you can't do this sort of thing.'

Frontline counter-terrorism officers wish for a world where parents look over what their kids are doing online. But in a workshop with parents in an inner-city ward, one of our police teams found that only 10 per cent of mums knew how to log on to the internet.

This is why we need an awful lot more of the sort of work pioneered by 7/7 survivor Sajda Mughal. Her work for the JAN Trust, founded in 1989, with programmes such as 'Web Guardians', helps women to develop technology skills that don't just help keep children safe but help unlock all sorts of barriers to exclusion. The programme does not come cheap and requires some thirty hours of work, but, in the world we're moving to, it is one of the best investments we can make.

There is also more we can do in schools. If we can't stop our children from exposure to the 'broadcast of evil', then we will need to help them become critical consumers; it will perhaps become as important as teaching Shakespeare – if not more so.

One of the most innovative digital companies in Birmingham, Maverick Television, has worked with one local school to understand the sort of material that will be needed. They argue that to take away the power of propaganda we have to demystify it; by explaining the calculated techniques used to create propaganda, we rob it of its power. That means helping children understand the creative techniques designed to trigger psychological mechanisms, like the way peer pressure rewards the brain, the diminished responsibility of the crowd, the magic of video game aesthetics, and what makes for charisma on camera – in other words, all the tricks that make up the mystery of showbiz. It means confronting young people with the realities of extremism and the horror of trauma. And it means, of course, helping explain the difference between peaceful and violent change.

Who will be the authors of all this? As Sajda Mughal put it to me, 'removing material doesn't work. People will just find it elsewhere, like on the dark web, if they're really looking'. The solution, therefore, has to be a flood of good material to counteract the bad. We need to multiply and amplify those voices, like Abdullah-X, splitting apart the extremist's ideology and behaviour.[104] We need many more tricks, like Facebook's scanning tool, which identifies those 'falling into the orbit of jihadists, and messages them with information for reformed extremists'.[105] We need a widespread narrative – 'counter-speech' – that knocks down the arguments of extremists and that we encourage our children to creatively co-produce and use to flood the digital channels to which they're connected.

Politicians need to play a role. At their best, they are our national storytellers. They have at their disposal the bully pulpit of Parliament. Their story cannot reinforce the 'clash of civilisations' worldview, which simply bolsters the mentality of our enemies. The media too has to strive for a better balance. It has to understand the role it plays in positioning people at the top of a slide into danger. We can't regulate the

---

104 Ezzeldeen Khalil, 'Counter-radicalization Moves into Social Media', *Jane's Intelligence Review*, 5 November 2015.

105 'Facebook Helps Pull Would-be Jihadists Back from the Brink', *The Times*, 15 September 2015.

press to do that, but we can influence who the press happens to be. The media industry is unbelievably white, especially at the top. A more diverse industry might sell more newspapers.

And finally, we could perhaps spend our money better. Lobbing a few Brimstone missiles around in Syria costs around £1 million a mission. Frankly, we should debate whether we have the balance of spending right. Could more money be better spent on charities such as JAN Trust's Web Guardians, which teaches parents to spot the warning signs in their children's online habits? The war against extremism is a generational struggle. But as Boy S proves, we need to be careful not to fight the last war against extremist preachers in the backrooms of mosques – but through the digital battle now at hand.

CHAPTER 7

PEACE IN THE POISONED CAULDRON

There are few better places to survey the 'new Middle East' than the top of the Al Bidda Tower in Qatar's downtown Doha. While the sun blazes high over the Persian Gulf, bouncing off a burgeoning forest of shiny skyscrapers, you have a beautiful view through the triangular steel windows of the elegant corniche, lined with a six-lane highway, stretching along the teal-blue bay to Doha Port. These are the headquarters of the Supreme Committee for Delivery and Legacy, otherwise known as Qatar's 2022

World Cup delivery team. In the lobby, huge screens count down the days, hours and seconds to kick-off on 18 December 2022, Qatar's National Day.

Qatar's Emirs are determined to put the tiny country on the map as one of the world's great hubs. The once sleepy home to the Gulf's pearl-fishers is now the master of the world's greatest gas fields. Its former ruler, Sheikh Hamad bin Khalifa Al Thani, created Al Jazeera, built up Qatar Airways and founded one of the world's most important sovereign wealth funds, the Qatar Investment Authority, with $100 billion invested in ventures such as the Shard, Heathrow Airport and Paris Saint-Germain FC. The tiny nation hosts world dialogues from the Doha trade talks to the Hamas–Fatah peace negotiations, and routes supplies to rebellions in both Syria and Libya. With the 2022 World Cup, it's set to host one of the greatest shows on earth and is pouring money into the project faster than it bubbles from its oil and gas fields: a staggering £150 billion will go into infrastructure, including a new rail network, hotels and roads, ahead of the tournament, dwarfing the £9.3 billion the UK spent on the 2012 London Olympics.[106] The head of the delivery team, Hassan Al Thawadi, is very clear about the Sultanate's ambitions: 'Bringing the World Cup here is a very big step and a pioneering step. The opportunities that come out of the World Cup here will open the doors and open minds about this region.'[107] It's a point that was underlined when I met Yasir Al Jamal, the Arsenal fan charged with actually delivering the project: 'We want to bring the world to the Middle East; we want to foster a new understanding of the region. We want to use it as a catalyst.' Despite all the World Cup's problems, it's an admirable vision – and it is a vision we need to support.

To defeat the extremists who want to kill us, we have to destroy the idea that there is some epic 'clash

---

106 https://www.theguardian.com/football/2015/nov/14/qatar-world-cup-200-billion-dollar-gamble

107 http://www.fifa.com/worldcup/news/y=2015/m=2/news=al-thawadi-a-world-cup-in-qatar-will-open-doors-and-minds-2532193.html

of civilisations' between Islam and the West. In fact, Islam and the West should be united in an alliance of the civilised against a cult: the heretical, totalitarian theocrats who 'love death as we love life' and wish to wipe out the freedom of Muslims, Jews and Christians alike to worship as our individual faith moves us. The imperative in our foreign policy, therefore, must be to build, sustain and advance this new coalition of the willing. And it will not be easy.

The region remains 'cursed with oil' and cut deep by the three seminal divisions of our time: between Israel and Palestine, between Sunni and Shi'ite, between India and Pakistan across the disputed line of control in Kashmir. Globally, oil states are 50 per cent more likely to be authoritarian, and a quarter of all oil states are embroiled in civil war.[108] Oil funded Iraq's invasion of Kuwait, Libya's support for terrorists, Iranian support for Hamas and Hezbollah and the rise of ISIS.

---

108 'How to End the Oil Curse', *Foreign Affairs*, 3 June 2016.

When I first backpacked through Jerusalem during the first intifada in 1989, I was shocked at little kids throwing stones at me on the Temple Mount. Twenty-five years later, on the streets of Ramallah in the West Bank, those children are Palestinian adults who remain profoundly disillusioned with the prospects for peace. In Ramallah, I've heard loud and clear how today, aspirational middle-class Palestinians are resigned and resentful, losing hope for a two-state solution in the Middle East. They're asking themselves whether, in reality, a one-state solution is the inevitable outcome – and so, why not wait for that; give up on a fabled two-state solution of Israel and Palestine side by side, and settle instead for a 'greater Israel', where Palestinians will become the majority?

Five hundred miles west of Palestine, secure in the diplomatic quarter, is the British High Commission in Pakistan. Its architecture is an acquired taste: 'Brutalised concrete was never really was my cup of tea,' said one British High Commissioner on my last stay; 'a bit like the South Bank', we agreed. The 'state quarters' on the first floor, overlooking a large, if slightly yellowing lawn, are fronted by a magnificent north-facing balcony, which stretches around the embassy affording a fabulous view of the irrevocably romantic Margalla Hills that stretch off east to the Himalayas. These are the mountains through which the Line of Control divides Kashmir between the 'nuclear neighbours' India and Pakistan. Confronting its giant neighbour, Pakistan has opted to spend a vast slice of its national wealth on security, shattering the funds available for development.

Between Palestine and Pakistan lies the 1,500 years of conflict between Sunni and Shi'ite. Across the abyss of this ancient divide, Saudi Arabia now confronts the new Iran. Iran's strategic alliances with the Assad regime in Syria and Lebanon's Hezbollah have strengthened the 'Shi'ite crescent'. Iran actively backs Hamas, the Houthis in Yemen, the Shi'ite in Bahrain and 'non-state actors' across every regional war zone, such as the Shi'ite militia groups in Iraq. These players are stronger than ever, and Iran, along with a newly assertive Russia, has become so confident, it is able to field frontline commanders in both Syria and Iraq.

The great powers that are left – Egypt, Jordan and Saudi Arabia – lack confidence in the 'American security umbrella'. They are more inclined to resort to force of their own, as we now see with every Saudi cluster bomb dropped in Yemen. The new Saudi regime, led by the eighty-year-old King Salman who acceded to the throne in 2015, is determined to present a tough front. Within months of his accession, the King conducted the largest mass execution since the 1980s, including Sheikh Nimr al-Nimr, one of the region's most prominent Shi'ite clerics. It was, said the Iranians, 'a crime' that was 'part of a criminal pattern by this treacherous family'.

In this boiling, poisoned cauldron – the birthplace of civilisation – the old regional system is at breaking point. The modern Arab states are collapsing; little help has been offered to Lebanon and Palestine to build strong new states of their own. Syria, Iraq and

Libya all became home to dictators, who struggled to offer progress to their people and then suffered catastrophic Western intervention. And the brutal testimony to the international community's inability to act are the half a million people who lie dead in Syria, the ten million who have lost their homes, and the eight million refugees, many now camped in Turkey or dying in the waters of the Aegean, drowning without life jackets as their inflatable dinghies capsize.

In the long term our best defence against a fanatical Middle East is a flourishing Middle East. Today, the biggest countries in the Middle East – Egypt, Turkey and Iran; each home to around eighty million people – are poor. The average Egyptian is about as wealthy as the average citizen in Swaziland. The average Iranian is seven times poorer than the average Israeli. The average Turk is as wealthy as a citizen of Suriname.[109] The cancer of poverty and inequality is as dangerous as any religious division. And now the low long-term oil

---

109 These comparisons made on basis of nominal GDP per capita.

price is fast becoming an existential threat to regional stability. Today, in many of the Gulf states, 60–80 per cent of people are employed by the public sector. Yet collapsing oil tax revenues means Arab countries can no longer afford this. The IMF forecasts that by 2021, unemployment among the big oil exporters could rise by three million people. That might mean a third of new entrants to the jobs market will be unemployed.[110]

Two stories from either end of the Middle East illustrate the challenge ahead.

An hour's ferry ride from Spain takes you to Morocco and the spectacular coast road, up to the Rif Mountains. The road winds round the red mountainsides like an old goat track. The land seems undivided, dotted with giant haystacks like yurts, of the sort van Gogh used to paint in southern France. The towns are like towns across the East. A strip of road. Cubist blocks a couple of stories high. Sun-scorched concrete

---

110 Oil exporters include: Gulf Cooperation Council nations, Algeria plus Iran, Iraq, Libya and Yemen. See, IMF, 'Learning to Live With Cheaper Oil', 2016, p. 36.

painted a shade of buttermilk. A mosque with a tall rectangular tower, edged in apple green, with a tiny tower perched on top. Children and old ladies in Berber dress ride donkeys and, by the roadside, there's a booming retail trade in walnuts, prickly pears – and marijuana. Outside village after village, young men whistle down cars, holding up two fingers in a victory sign and offering Moroccan black. Down the wadis cut through the rock, dense patches of the distinctive leaf grow everywhere. The area under cannabis crops in the Rif mountains is nearly 50,000 hectares, producing, at the last estimate, 760 tons of the stuff. Are we surprised? Wealth per head in Morocco is a little over £2,000.[111]

Meanwhile, over 4,000 miles away in Iraq, the military advance against ISIS is under threat from economic collapse. Every political leader I met in the Kurdistan Region in Iraq was blunt: Kurdistan's

---

111 http://www.emcdda.europa.eu/topics/pods/cannabis-resin-market-europe

economy is in crisis. Some 70 per cent of workers are on the public payroll. Electricity is free. The government's bills are big, but taxes are non-existent. The banks don't work. Inward investment is ensnared in red tape. And when the oil price collapsed last year, the government's budget fell through the floor. In a bust-up with Baghdad, cash has been slashed to Kurdistan, just as a wave of 250,000 refugees arrived, along with over a million internally displaced people fleeing ISIS and Shi'ite militias in the south. Nearly 6,000 development projects are stalled and people – including the Peshmerga – haven't been paid for months. We have brave allies in the fight against ISIS, but bravery doesn't buy bullets. It took a *year* for the British to replenish ammunition for the small number of heavy machine guns we supplied, and Peshmerga deaths are higher for lack of such effective tools. This level of poverty and insecurity is dangerous.

Naturally, many British voters will want to turn away. There are plenty of politicians who offer a prospect of pulling up the drawbridge, like Nigel Farage's infamous 'Breaking Point' poster of the 'hordes flood-ing in', so reminiscent of Nazi-era propaganda.

But we cannot walk away from the Islamic world of the Middle East, central and south-east Asia, because our enemies believe they are at war with the West. Unlike the Taliban, ISIS wants to grow; as its slogan says, 'This Khalifa will have no borders, inshallah, only fronts.' You cannot defend a goal by standing on the goal-line. We will always have to engage on a forward line. The digital battlefront does not stop magically at the white cliffs of Dover. It can be reached from a smartphone in the inner city.

Just as important, in today's globalised world, our economies and our societies are deeply intercon-nected. Our exports to the Middle East total £22.6 billion,[112] with imports running at about the same value. That is a lot of jobs. The Middle East is our third biggest export market after the US and Europe.

---

112 Figures are for 2014. Excludes India. Exports are principally with
     the United Arab Emirates, Saudi Arabia, Egypt, Israel, Morocco,
     Qatar and Turkey. Source: House of Commons library figures.

We sell as much there as we do to India and China put together. In 2013, we invested over £5 billion in the region, most of it in the UAE. And more important than the money are people. Not long after I became a minister in the Home Office, I was chatting about the world with a senior counter-terrorism official; he said something I'll never forget: 'Today, Pakistan is to Britain, what Ireland was to Britain for centuries.' He is right. The movement of our citizens back and forth to south-east Asia today is little different from the movement of my grandparent's generation back and forth between Britain and my ancestral home of Ireland. We are entwined with the Islamic world, because our citizens are entwined. And we are richer for it.

But, if we are to help foster the alliance of the civilised against the cult, we have to recognise that we have some history to deal with. A history that fosters suspicion of our motives – which our recent policy has only reinforced.

Much of our history in the region was defined by

securing the 'passage to India' and the oil fields we found along the way.

After the near disaster of the Indian mutiny in 1857–58, the Crown took direct control of the sub-continent, and thereafter India rapidly became the hub on which Victoria's global system turned. Indian troops provided the Empire with a mobile force deployable almost anywhere on earth.[113] As Europe and America raised tariffs to close their markets, cotton exports to India became critically important,[114] as the country became Britain's single

---

113 Indian troops served in China (1860), Abyssinia (1868), Perak (1875–76), Baluchistan, Malta, Cyprus, Afghanistan, Egypt, Burma, Nyasa, Mombasa, Uganda and Sudan.

114 Cotton sold to India made up 30 per cent of cotton export growth between 1820 and 1850, by which time India was consuming a fifth of British cotton goods. Between 1870 and 1913, India rose from third to first place among Britain's export markets. British textiles made up one-third of the country's imports, and Britain's positive balance of trade with India was equivalent to the trade deficit with America. By 1910, Britain's balance of trade with the US was a deficit of £50 million, and with Europe of £45 million. The trade surplus of £60 million with India, and £13 million with Australia, was therefore critical to Britain's settling of its accounts, financing over 80 per cent of the US–Europe trade

most important export market and, crucially, India became a huge market for British capital. By 1909, Lord Curzon could remark with some justice that India was now 'the determining influence of every considerable movement in British power to the east and south of the Mediterranean'.[115]

Securing the route to India triggered the creation of a vast security zone stretching from Gibraltar to the eastern borders of Persia, the strongest official 'interest' in Britain's world system,[116] and that meant Egypt became of vital interest, especially after the creation of the Suez Canal. When Egypt's Khedive was running low on cash, Disraeli snapped up the chance to buy the canal in 1875, and Britain acquired a direct stake in the nation. But when the Khedive's

---

deficit. Furthermore, much of India's overseas trade was in the hands of British shippers and merchants; a third of the Empire's trade outside Britain passed through India's seaports.

115 Robin J. Moore, 'Imperial India, 1858–1914', pp. 442–3.

116 John Darwin, *The Empire Project: The Rise and Fall of the British World-System, 1830–1970* (Cambridge University Press: 2009), p. 622.

son began to lose control of both the country's security and its finances – including payments on British loans – Gladstone agreed to invade. At 7 a.m. on 11 July 1882, the British navy commenced a ten-hour bombardment of Alexandria. Two months later, the Highland Brigade silently marched through the flat desert between Alexandria and Cairo. At dawn, the bagpipes struck up and the British attacked the capital, while forty Royal Navy warships secured the Suez Canal. Egypt was occupied as a 'temporary expedient', an assurance the British issued no fewer than sixty-six times between 1882 and 1922.[117]

Like Egypt, Iran's misfortune was to lie along the route to India, but worse, to sit atop unlimited wealth. Here, some of the first great civilisations were founded.[118] Here was the cradle of the first

---

117 See Niall Ferguson, *Empire* (Penguin, 2004) p. 235.

118 Five centuries before Christ, on the desert borders of southern Iran, giants of the ancient world – Cyrus, Darius, Xerxes – built Persepolis, one of the first great capitals of human civilisation, resplendent with giant statues of winged bulls guarding the Gate of All Nations, through which marched the vassal kings of

revealed religion, the Zoroastrians and the cruci-
ble of Shi'ite Islam. Like Egypt, the British sought to
'protect' Iran, to protect the road to India from the
northern threat of Russia. Rights to build a telegraph
line were acquired in 1857. Fourteen years later, Baron
Julius de Reuter hit the jackpot, acquiring, for next to
nothing, the right to run the nation's industry, build
the railways, irrigate the farms, mine the land and
print the money. It was, said Lord Curzon, 'the most
complete and extraordinary surrender of the entire
industrial resources of a kingdom into foreign hands
that has probably never been dreamed of, much less
accomplished, in history'.[119] After seven patient
years exploring, William Knox D'Arcy's team struck

---

their wide empire to pay homage in the vast Hall of Audience.
Here Elamites, Arachosians, Armenians, Ethiopians, Somalis,
Thracians, Arabs, Indians and Assyrians came to lay tributes
before the king of kings, an emperor who could field armies of
180,000 men and controlled an empire, connected by roads,
bridges, uniform coinage, tax and post, that stretched from
Greece to Egypt, Libya and east across the Caucasus to the banks
of the Indus.

119   Stephen Kinzer, *All the Shah's Men* (John Wiley, 2003), Chapter 3.

the greatest oil field ever found at 4 a.m. on 26 May 1908.[120] The British government quickly moved in.

Because oil burns four times more efficiently than coal, Winston Churchill took the decision in 1912 to switch the engines of the Royal Navy from coal to oil. It became vital, said the Admiralty, for Britain 'to obtain the undisputed control of the greatest amount of petroleum that we can'.[121] That, concluded Admiral Hankey, required control of the Middle East: 'the power that controls the oil lands of Persia and Mesopotamia will control the source of supply of the majority of the liquid fuel of the future,' wrote Hankey. 'This control must be absolute and there must be no foreign interests involved in it of any sort.'[122] The British government took 51 per cent of the new Anglo-Persian oil company, which drilled, built pipelines and created the world's largest oil refinery on the desert

---

120 Kinzer, ibid.

121 James Barr, *A Line in the Sand* (Simon & Schuster, 2011), p. 65.

122 Barr, ibid., p. 66.

island of Abadan. It was, said Winston Churchill, 'a prize from fairy land beyond our wildest dreams'.

Iraq was to suffer the same fate, for the same ruthless rationale. After the First World War, Britain and France settled a border sketched across the Middle East, based on a design suggested in Downing Street on 16 December 1915 by Sir Mark Sykes, who proposed his infamous 'line in the sand' to the War Cabinet with the words: 'I should like to draw a line from the "e" in acre to the last "k" in Kirkuk.'[123] The Sykes–Picot line, as it was known, was enshrined in an Anglo-French diplomatic deal signed on 16 May 1916, leaving Britain in command of a vast zone stretching from southern Iraq to Baghdad to Haifa, with Palestine under international control. After the war, Britain and France conspired to frustrate the dreams of the Arab nationalists. Arab ambitions for Syrian independence were surrendered to French ambitions in return for a free hand to rule Palestine,

---

123 Quoted, Barr, ibid.

and the French agreed to bend the Sykes–Picot line north of Kirkuk, allowing British control of Mosul and its legendary oil fields, where oil was discovered on 14 October 1927 in a surge so big it killed two drillers. By 1940, the Turkish Petroleum Company[124] was producing 4 million tons of oil a year, enough to supply Britain's entire Mediterranean fleet, through a pipeline dubbed by *Time* magazine 'the carotid artery of the British empire'.[125]

The interwar years were ugly, creating a permanent suspicion of Britain and France in the region, and helping inspire the Islamist political theory that fuels extremism today. A succession of coups and counter-coups in Iraq eventually brought Saddam Hussein's Ba'ath Party to power in Iraq in 1963, which by 1970 had established itself as Iraq's dominant force.

Meanwhile, Iranians were living in poverty while

---

124 Jointly owned by Anglo-Persian, Royal Dutch Shell, Compagnie française des pétroles and the Near East Development Corporation.

125 Barr, op. cit., p. 163.

the country's oil, harvested by the British-controlled Anglo Iranian Oil Company, the most profitable company in the world, helped power the Royal Navy ships that policed a global empire. Iranian patience finally snapped in 1951, when Mohammad Mosaddegh, the high-minded son of a Qajar princess, was swept to power with a mandate to nationalise the Anglo Iranian Oil Company. He was a man, as one European newspaper put it, who 'would rather be fried in Persian oil than make the slightest concession to the British'.[126] A bitter standoff followed that Britain looked set to lose. But Britain found a new ally in President Eisenhower, whose Secretary of State John Forster Dulles and new head of the CIA Allan Dulles were convinced by MI6's Christopher Montague Woodhouse that an independent Iran would give Moscow a dangerous new ally. And so, over the course of 1953, the CIA executed Operation Ajax with spectacular success, triggering a popular

126 Quoted in Kinzer, op. cit.

uprising against Mosaddegh and the ascent of the pro-Western Mohammed Reza Shah to the Peacock Throne. It was the regime that lasted until the Iranian Revolution of 1979.

Just for good measure, the British were unable to leave a sustainable foundation for an independent Palestine. It had been declared in 1917 that 'His Majesty's Government view with favour the establishment in Palestine of a national home for the Jewish people, and will use their best endeavours to facilitate this object.'[127] Throughout the 1930s, British rule in Palestine proved tough. Jewish immigration and land purchase from poor, indebted Arab farmers raised tensions, and as the violence escalated, Jewish settlers began to take self-defence into their own hands. Successive commissions proposed various divisions of land that never proved satisfactory, and so, in the face of escalating violence, the British government

---

127 This was the famous Balfour Declaration, which was, in fact, designed to ward off French pressure for international administration of Palestine.

asked the new United Nations to opine. The General Assembly agreed a division of land between Israel and Palestine on 29 November 1947, and in May 1948, the last British forces left from Haifa. Hitherto, the Arabs had rejected all plans for partition as unfair and, in the same month that saw the departure of the British forces, the Arab invasion of Palestine inaugurated the first Arab-Israeli War.

It is this long history that should have inspired more care in our alliance with America against al Qaeda in Afghanistan and Saddam Hussein in Iraq. As the Chilcot report made clear, an unconditional subscription to American policy has not served us well. Nor has the doctrine of 'liberal interventionism' set out by Tony Blair in his 1998 speech in Chicago. Too often, we have seemed oblivious to our 130 years of history in the region defined by our colonial interests in India, oil and Israel, and our special relationship with America. It is this history that should have inspired extraordinary caution rather than the unconditional support to George W. Bush offered by Tony Blair. This is why we need to reset our policy abroad: we need to be realistic about our history, but ambitious for the future. Along with our determination to fight for Muslims' freedom of conscience should be a new determination to foster freedom to trade, to prosper, to grow. As the saying goes, we would not start from here. But for the future, there are some clear ideas that should guide our hand.

BLACK HOLE SUNS

CHAPTER 8

THE NEW SILK ROAD

First things first. We should accept that we'd have an awful lot more freedom to manoeuvre in our Middle Eastern policy if we were less dependent on foreign energy. Keeping more known fossil fuel reserves in the ground is a good thing; it's crucial to keeping global temperature increases to below the crucial 2 degrees Celsius. But energy independence would be awfully good for security too. Many ascribe America's new-found flexibility in the Middle East, at least in part, to the shale gas revolution, which means that America will be so self-sufficient in oil and gas that it need not import *any* by 2035.[128]

Once upon a time, Britain was 'energy independent'.[129] When the great oil and gas fields of the North Sea came fully online in 1981, Britain was a net *exporter of energy*. But North Sea production peaked in 1999, and since 2004 we have been importing substantial amounts of energy. Now, nearly half our energy comes from abroad.[130] Over 40 per cent of our coal comes from Russia and nearly half (45 per cent) of our crude oil comes from Norway, which also provides well over half our gas.[131]

A crucial strategic slice of our energy still comes from the Gulf: around a third of our crude

---

128 Michael Lind, 'The Wars That Really Are About the Oil', *Spectator Magazine*, 30 August 2014.

129 http://researchbriefings.parliament.uk/ResearchBriefing/Summary/SN04046#fullreport

130 In 2014, 46 per cent of energy used in the UK was imported, up sharply from the 2010 level.

131 2014 figures.

oil, and about a quarter of our gas. That's £6.5 billion of energy from the area – two-thirds of it from Saudi Arabia, Qatar and Kuwait. So, developing energy independence and encouraging a new filigree of supply lines, north and south of the Black Sea, and reducing Europe's reliance on Russian gas routes, would buy us an awful lot more freedom.

The challenge is that Gulf fossil fuel is now, relatively, cheap as chips – and this may not change for some years. Slower global growth means lower energy demand. The lifting of sanctions on Iran means new oil supplies have come online along with Iran's slice of the world's largest natural energy store, the gas fields deep beneath the Persian Gulf. Iran's South Pars field is thought to hold at least 325 trillion cubic feet of natural gas – enough to supply all of Europe's needs for the next sixteen years – and could be online within five years. Liquefied natural gas prices have already more than halved since 2014, and to hold their share of global markets,

Saudi Arabia has to keep on pumping, keeping oil prices low.[132] That means there's much less incentive to pump cash into new non-carbon sources like renewables or nuclear, plus new pipelines. Yet, strategically it would make an awful lot of sense to do so.

THE BLEEDING HEART OF IT

If we want to really prove there is no 'clash of civilisations', then we have to make progress on what is widely described as the 'bleeding heart of it': a safe, secure two-state solution between Israel and Palestine.

One former British ambassador to the region put it to me, 'The Israel/Palestine conflict is not a religious one. It's about power, land, security … competing claims, competing narratives.' But anyone who has spent time in Palestine knows how quickly politics

---

132 Andrew Critchlow, 'Iran to Trigger Natural Gas Race with Qatar in Persian Gulf', *Daily Telegraph*, 8 October 2015.

dissolves into religion: 'It can degenerate into a religious conflict,' the former ambassador went on. 'Jewish control of Muslim access to al-Aqsa Mosque (the third holiest place in Islam), and on the other hand, the religious ideology of violent settlers who believe that God gave them Judea and Samaria [today's West bank], so it's their duty to expel Palestinians.'

In my visits over the years, Israeli politicians and military figures have described a world without hope. The economy of the West Bank is stuttering; its trade is jammed by the security walls around it, weakening the strength of the Palestinian Authority. Too often, money now runs dry for the 160,000–170,000 Palestinian public servants – who have bank loans, credit cards, mortgages – including 60,000 police and soldiers. With guns.

From Gaza, the rocket attacks continue, defeated only by the missile defence system, Iron Dome. From Egypt, the risk of the 'tunnel economy' to the Sinai remains. Few think there is a solution – just methods of living with friction. Once there was at least a little optimism that a deal of returning land to the Palestinians was possible. But few see how a Palestinian leader – especially a leader forced to compete with Hamas – could settle a deal that forbade a right of return for the Palestinian diaspora scattered around the world. As one Israeli politician put it to me, 'How can leaders say: "I sold you out. You can never come home." People blame leaders. But if leaders can't deliver the people, it becomes a bit of an empty argument.'

Talk about peace with military officers and the constant refrain is: 'How do we make progress when there is no trust on either side?' There is no sense that because politics lacks the capacity to deal with the issues, then alternative channels – in business, in civil society – should develop. And so, Israeli politicians anticipate their opposite numbers will seek to do more through international bodies such as the UN. Yet, the total absence of a political framework for talks makes it harder to put in place the mechanisms – what someone once described to me as 'mutually coordinated unilateral steps' – that might afford a little economic relief. And week by week, under the security umbrella of the Israeli Defence Force, Israeli settlements advance throughout the biblical lands. Among Israeli civil society, there is great sympathy for the Palestinians, and hostility towards settlements. But many Israelis fear that the Palestinians want all the land, not just the West Bank and Gaza. Which is why they continue to elect right-wing governments.

A few miles east of Jerusalem, in one of the posher restaurants in Ramallah on the West Bank one evening, I was lucky enough to have dinner with one of the most experienced Palestinian negotiators. Aside from a decent mixed grill, it was a profoundly depressing evening. There is little faith that Israeli voters will pressure their leaders to sue for peace, and even less confidence in the Americans. The process sponsored by John Kerry was seen to cost land, money and credibility. And the thirty-seven standing ovations given by Congress to Israeli Prime Minister Benjamin Netanyahu hardly went unnoticed.

The critical strategic risk is the disillusionment

of young people; a secular, nationalist people turning to the forces of a global caliphate, rendering it impossible to form a stable core in the region. Young leaders are the key, but many 'have drifted off' into business or civil society. They have got on with life and kept apart from politics. The younger generation of Palestinians is giving up on hope. Belief is growing in 'hanging on for a one-state solution'. 'The key now', said my dinner partner, 'is to sustain hope – and that's why Europe has to plough its own path now. Not outsource it to the US.'

The simplest, starkest views are to be found with the people struggling for the quiet miracle of a normal life. The old road from Jerusalem to Jericho, where the Good Samaritan helped the man who had been mugged and left to die, takes you through the Jordan Rift Valley that stretches from Eilat in the south of Israel, all the way north into Syria. Here, Jesus spent his forty days in the wilderness, on the great dead flat plain, running to the Dead Sea. Here the rain runs down the hills, into the irrigation canals dating back

to Roman times. And here I stopped at a run-down
Bedouin settlement, not much more than a shepherd's
camp in a riverbed, a shelter from the wind that blows
down the green and brown valley. Mukhtar's house
was made of mud and stones with wooden frames, and
blue tarpaulin-covered pens for sheep and goats. His
family were originally from near Hebron, and today he
boasts a flock of about 100 sheep, nursed in a trade that
is, he smiled, 'as old as time'.

Against the skyline, not far off, is Jabal al-Qarantal,
the Mount of Temptation, where the devil tempted
Jesus. Today, a dodgy cable-car goes to the summit,
and the top is occupied by troops; 'Not so holy any
more,' as one of my guides put it. The Jordan Valley
should be the bread basket of Palestine, but instead,
farmers struggle for water.

Private Palestinian land is protected. But 'common land', of which there was much in the time of
the Ottomans, is not. Property rights of those herders who drifted up from the Negev were based on
old understandings. And so, under a potpourri

of Ottoman, Jordanian and British mandate law, new settlers are executing what is tantamount to enclosure of the commons. Military law overrides everything, and the effect is simple. Palestinian families can't move their homes to the top of riverbanks. So their homes flood. Concrete roofs or floors are prohibited, as that would mean a 'permanent settlement'. Many buildings are liable for demolition. If a system cannot even provide security for poor herders, then what hope is there? Until there is security that unlocks justice in a two-state solution, that guarantees Israeli and Palestinian security alike, there will be little peace. Britain, thank God, is no longer an imperial power. But as the first architect of the current mess, we must never fail to play a proactive part in a Europe that helps broker answers.

THE ARCHIPELAGO OF TOLERANCE

Beyond Israel/Palestine, there is of course a new

balance of power now taking shape. The region's rising appetite for democracy and the world's declining appetite for oil has set a stage on which the United States is less assertive while both Russia and China are seeking to advance.

Caught in the middle, the states sketched on a map by the British and the French – Iraq and Syria – home to both Sunni, Shi'ites and others, are struggling, while regional powers – Iran, Turkey and Saudi Arabia – are stretching out, arming a plethora of highly dangerous 'non-state actors' who use terror to reshape both regional power and the global narrative.

As America's alliance with Saudi Arabia has loosened and Iran has been cautiously admitted back into the global system, the risk now is that the old Sunni–Shi'ite rivals double down on their old 'faith race'. Iran's leader has declared that 'Israel must be pushed into the sea'. It's a country that has sought nuclear weapons and the capacity to enrich uranium, supplies Hamas and Hezbollah, boasts Shahab-3 medium-range weapons at home and tens of thousands of rockets ready to fire from Lebanon, and deploys senior Iranian Revolutionary Guards in the chaos of Syria to direct defeat of Sunni-dominated ISIS.

Meanwhile, Saudi Arabia has patched up its alliances with its neighbours on the Gulf Cooperation Council (GCC), designated Iran-backed Hezbollah a terrorist group, and intensified the bombing of Shi'ite Houthi rebels in Yemen.[133] Much now depends on the evolution of Iranian democracy, where there are signs at least of progress by moderate forces,[134] and our ability to check Saudi Arabia's export of extreme ideology and arms.

Given this divide, we may not make much progress persuading some sort of united regional forces there

---

133 http://english.alarabiya.net/en/views/news/middle-east/ 2016/03/07/The-Role-of-Iranian-moderates-in-the-crisis-with-the-Gulf.html

134 Mohsen Milani, 'How Iran's Moderates Triumphed', *Foreign Affairs*, 4 March 2016.

to adopt 'Western' goals, such as a variant of secular rule or disposing of evil dictators. But that should not stop us trying. Strategically, however, it is vital that amid the rivalries of the great powers – Saudi Arabia, Iran, Turkey, Israel, Egypt – we strengthen the 'archipelago of tolerance' that stretches the length of the region. It's an archipelago of calm, patient nations such as Morocco, Tunisia and Jordan, along with smaller Gulf states including Oman and Qatar, urgently seeking to modernise, plus regions like Kurdistan, where a culture of pluralism and tolerance runs so deep, it helps define the local sense of patriotism.

Here there are positive signs of change, from the Moroccan king's appetite to devolve power within a new Constitution, to Jordan's successful bid to become an associate member of the Council of Europe. This new approach may entail accepting that Iraq is never likely to work as a functional state. As one senior minister in Kurdistan said to me:

Every time I go to Baghdad I see a more Shi'ite

Baghdad. The suburbs are a mess; it is disgraceful. Full of anger and rage and hate. We're not optimistic about the Sunni regions either – there's no leadership. It's broken up into a myriad of tribes. Sunni devolution is the only answer. The days of controlling Iraq from Baghdad are gone. Iraq – I don't see it any more.

Another added that Iraq was always a 'mosaic country that never gelled together. It was held together by force. If you want to be united you need to be united by agreement.' In the Ashti refugee camp, I heard first-hand how ISIS had destroyed 10 per cent of towns – but Shi'ite militias had finished the job.

THE NEW SILK ROAD

Strategically, the greatest long-term risk is today's economic weakness that curses the land from the Maghreb and Middle East. Over the past ten years, we have spent nearly £15 billion in aid to countries in the Middle East and south-east Asia – about half of it in India and Pakistan, around £3 billion in Afghanistan, and £2.6 billion in Iraq. But there has been no grand vision to this; it's just good old-fashioned development spending. There is no strategic intent behind it, no grand effort to transform our economic relationship, or to foster new institutions that connect us, or to build infrastructure that might help old countries trade and prosper.

And that is why we should take a lesson from China, and a thirty-two-container train that arrived in Tehran in February.

Travelling over 6,000 miles in fourteen days from China's eastern Zhejiang province through Kazakhstan and Turkmenistan, the train shaved a month off the time it takes to move from Shanghai to the Iranian port of Bandar Abbas by sea.[135] 'The arrival

---

135 https://www.theguardian.com/business/2016/feb/15/chinas-silk-road-revival-steams-ahead-as-cargo-train-arrives-in-iran

in Tehran of the train in less than a fortnight has been an unprecedented achievement,' said Mohsen Pour Seyed Aghaei, president of the Islamic Republic of Iran Railways company, who boasted that the train had outstripped 'truck and road transport' and demonstrated the great advantage of the route. The new connections are not only by rail, but also sea; early in 2016, an Iranian container ship, the *Perarin*, arrived in Guangxi in southern China, delivering 978 containers from a number of countries along the maritime route.

These are the first fruits of China's One Belt, One Road (OBOR) design for a new silk road that connects the sixty-five Eurasian countries and 4.4 billion people[136] along the ancient filigree of roads described with such wonder by Marco Polo.

Launched in 2013, the plans encompass connections from China's coast to Europe through the South China Sea and the Indian Ocean to the South

---

136 https://www.sc.com/BeyondBorders/china-one-belt-one-road/

Pacific. On land, a new Eurasian land bridge will run through economic corridors to Russia, central Asia and Indochina – buttressed by a dazzling array of diplomatic mechanisms: the Shanghai Cooperation Organisation, ASEAN plus China, APEC, the Asia–Europe Meeting, Asia Cooperation Dialogue, the China-Arab States Cooperation Forum, the China Gulf Cooperation Council Strategic Dialogue, to name but a few.[137]

China's foreign minister set out the principles in Iran earlier this year:

The Silk Road Economic Belt, in general, has three dimensions: First, connectivity. The goal is to closely connect as much of Eurasian continent as possible by rail, road, air and network to create basic conditions for development. Second, production capacity cooperation. This is to raise the

---

137 See Foreign Language Press, 'Vision and Actions on Jointly Building Silk Road Economic Belt', March 2015.

level of industrialisation and enhance the capacity for development for various countries through
win–win cooperation. And third, cultural and
people-to-people exchange.[138]

Crucially, OBOR has become an umbrella for a basket
of 1,000 projects, including the Yanbu petrochemical
refinery in Saudi Arabia, an industrial park in Oman,
a 'silk city' project in Kuwait and development programmes around several islands. China has said it
will allocate $62 billion from its foreign exchange
reserves to three state-owned 'policy banks'.[139]

The programme is obviously good for China's
self-interest. By 2030, China will become the world's
largest energy consumer; 52 per cent of China's
oil comes from the Gulf region[140] and as China's

---

138 http://www.tehrantimes.com/news/402740/Chinese-FM-Iran-
has-long-standing-ties-with-us

139 https://www.rt.com/business/332631-china-iran-train-arrives/

140 M. Singh, 'China's Middle East Tour', *Foreign Affairs*, 24 January
2016.

economy matures, the nation needs to export surplus industrial capacity such as steel and cement.

The anchor of the plan may prove China's connection to Iran. In January 2016, China's President Xi Jinping was the first to arrive in Iran after the sanctions lift to sign plans to boost trade to £420 billion over the next decade (about five times the size of UK–China trade ambitions). But China has been deepening relationships throughout the region: not only was China part of the Iran nuclear talks, but its naval units joined Russians for exercises in the Med (in May 2015), and will soon boast a base in Djibouti.

It's an approach we should learn from. The closest any European has come to this kind of design was President Sarkozy's efforts to transform what Eurocrats called the 'Barcelona process', and create a grand new Union of the Mediterranean: a sprawling intergovernmental organisation that brought together the twenty-eight European Union Member States and fifteen countries from the southern and eastern shores of the Mediterranean. It was mishandled from the start, and ended with a rather random range of projects from fighting pollution in the Mediterranean to better anti-terrorism coordination to cultural exchanges for scientists and students.[141]

We should now reflect on Sarkozy's mistakes and build, not some new bureaucracy, but an ambitious silk road vision of our own, lining up development spending and bank finance behind a shared programme to develop trade infrastructure, spur innovation, encourage enterprise and ultimately trade, safe in the knowledge that countries which trade more, grow faster. For years, we've lacked a shared vision for peaceful trade and growth with the Middle East that hasn't centred on arms or oil. It's time for us to move on.

---

141 http://www.nytimes.com/2008/07/06/world/europe/06iht-sarko.4.14279170.html?_r=0

EASTERN DEMOCRACY

During my last hours in Iraq, I wandered through the tight alleys and lanes of the ancient Citadel, the great mass of old mud-brown brick on the bluff above Erbil, overlooking the town square. Here, it is said, men and women have lived continuously for the past 5,000 years in the oldest inhabited city in the world. A stone's throw away is a jam-packed tea-shop, which opened in the 1950s, now run by Omar and his two brothers.

Omar started work at the age of seven, inherited the business from his dad, and today its tall ceilings allow the smoke of the water-pipes to rise, and the walls are plastered with framed pictures of the heroes of the Kurdish resistance. The Kurds have a saying: 'The Kurds have no friends but the mountains', and here were the portraits of the men who had led a people on a long struggle for freedom. Omar showed me an old, faded picture of the first Cabinet of the Kingdom of Kurdistan, full of men with serious eyes and serious moustaches, which ran the region briefly before the

Sykes-Picot agreement, and before, Omar smiled, 'our good friends in Britain sold us out'.

'Here is real social democracy,' said a friend, looking around the bustling cafe. 'Everyone who comes in is an equal. Whether they are a minister or a worker. In here everyone is equal.' Here, working men mix with writers, authors and thinkers, writing columns. And after a game of dominos or backgammon, the conversations about politics begin. It's like the tea room at the House of Commons.

There is nothing 'un-Islamic' about democracy. By far the most common of the Islamist reservations about a democratic system centres on the 'sovereignty of the people' taken to contravene the idea that God alone is sovereign. And it's not 'democracy' but the idea of justice that resonates most with those who are sucked into violence; indeed, most Muslim fundamentalist parties call themselves the party of '*adl*' or 'justice' in Arabic. It was a well-established principle in the time of the prophet, in particular, the ideal community of Medina, that the people chose the well-guided Caliph. And for the younger generation today, the sentiments that powered the Arab Spring remain; as one Gulf ambassador put it to me: 'the heat that still smoulders under its ashes'. 'How can the young generation today be happy,' he said, 'when their resources have been stolen by mafias?'

Attempts to impose a Western-style Westminster democracy are doomed to failure. After 2003, US neoconservatives proposed 'the modernization' of the Arab World as their recipe for achieving counter-terrorism, global stability and national security goals. It was, as Francis Fukuyama[142] incisively observed, a disastrous mix of views; a concern with democracy, human rights, and a belief that US power could be used for moral purposes such as spreading democracy, if necessary, by force. It failed to appreciate both the Eastern struggle with the sheer speed of modernisation – and the role religion plays in both public *and* private life.

---

142 See Francis Fukuyama, *After the Neocons* (Profile, 2006).

In a country like Qatar, for instance, the older generation have watched their country change, in two generations, from a sleepy land of pearl-fishers to a nation where their grandchildren have first-world diseases such as obesity. They watched the first aeroplanes land. Their children worked hard to develop the country. Now, they worry that their grandchildren have it easy. In these worlds of new inter-generational division, the older generation is anxious for stability and tradition.

Western models of governance would always struggle in a world that treasures a unity between religion and public life. As the theologian Dr Karen Armstrong points out, it is only really in the West where religion has become a 'practice [that] is essentially private and hermetically sealed off from all secular activities'.[143] In other languages and cultures, religion refers to something much more encompassing: the Arabic

---

143 K. Armstrong, *Fields of Blood: Religion and History of Violence* (The Bodley Head, 2014), p. 2.

din, like the Sanskrit *dharma*, 'signifies a whole way of life' encompassing law, justice, morals and social life.

I met Dr Armstrong at the House of Commons to chat it over. 'Before Locke,' Dr Armstrong argues, 'there was no secularism.' Religion suffused all life, public and private. 'We required it [the separation of religion from public life] as a necessary condition of economy building – because you can't have people like the Church telling you to hold back on for example the process of invention and discovery. That independence of thought is a crucial ingredient of our modernisation.'

But our 'aggressive secularism', as Armstrong describes it, was never likely to get far in the Middle East, where from the 1930s, secularism came to be seen as a foreign ideal and an aggressive evil. Hence the long tradition of thinkers who sought to create an Islamic approach to modernity, from the inside.

If we want to promote 'rights' therefore across the Middle East, rather than simply impose our Westminster parliamentary democracy from the outset, we'd be better off rooting our appeal in the very Islamic ideal of justice, and, from an idea of justice, argue for the enlargement of rights and entitlements for every citizen, equally, under God. For instance, the right to survive and have good health, to be skilled, knowledgeable, and to have a good job with a sufficient income and aspirations for the future; to have a decent place to live, and to live free from fear or attack; to have a strong, supportive family life, and be part of a strong, active community; and to enjoy a healthy, sustainable natural environment around which you can move freely.

To make these rights a reality, our aid should go on helping build the wealth of *institutions* that deliver those realities every day. All too often, we forget the role of institutions in our own national story. As the late, great Nobel economist Douglass North proved, institutions are the key to economic progress.[144]

---

144 http://www.ppge.ufrgs.br/giacomo/arquivos/econ-crime-old/
north-1991.pdf

Look at Britain. Down the ages, there would have been no British miracle if it wasn't for great national institutions like the Royal Navy, the Royal Exchange, the Royal Courts of Justice, the Royal Society and our universities, the welfare state – and yes, Parliament, as a check against despotic rulers.[145]

These are the institutions we should help nurture and interconnect in partnerships with institutions across the world. A good model is the Academic City now built on the outskirts of Dubai, a sprawling 2,500-acre campus that is home to university research centres and partners such as Georgetown University, Texas A&M University, Virginia Commonwealth University and Cornell University's Weill Medical College.

Ultimately, democracy has always taken root when people feel they have something to lose and seek peaceful means to defend their rights and

---

145 See Liam Byrne, *Dragons: 10 Entrepreneurs Who Built Britain* (Head of Zeus, 2016).

entitlements, which are seen as the key to a better, more optimistic future. We've been building institutions for over six centuries. It's an extraordinary expertise we have to offer.

CONCLUSION: SELF-CONFIDENT IDEALISM

Today, we think of globalisation as something new. But it isn't. It was slowly invented along the trade roads and sea lanes that connected Europe to the Middle East and China beyond, from the very birth of towns and cities. Weaving East and West together were the silk roads and sea lanes first opened by Han emissaries in Roman times, through Samarkand, Isfahan and Herat to Europe, or along the coast of Indochina, around the Malay peninsula to the Bay of Bengal and Sri Lanka, through Egypt, up the Nile, to the Mediterranean.[146] The millennia of exchange between East and West has created the civilisation to which we are heirs.

'Rome's eyes', as the historian Peter Frankopan puts it, 'had been fixed on Asia from the moment it transformed itself from a republic into an empire.'[147] Our forebears created the extraordinary world that can still inspire wonder in the weathered sculptured stones and monuments in ruins, from Morocco's Volubilis on the plains before the Atlas Mountains to Baalbek in the foothills of Anti-Lebanon. Equally, the glory of the early Islamic caliphates owed much to 'Western' influence. As Amira Bennison puts it, 'The first caliphal dynasty, that of the Umayyads (661–750) presided over and fostered the birth of a new civilisation, that of Islam,

---

146 Some of the earliest description were laid out for the West by
     Marco Polo in his volume described as 'a book of great puzzles'
     by his best translator, Sir Henry Yule. Sir Henry Yule, *The Book of
     Ser Marco Polo* (London: John Murray, 1903), vol. 1, p. 1.

147 Peter Frankopan, *The Silk Roads: A New History of the World*
     (Bloomsbury, 2015), p. 26.

which imbibed the heady aromas of Greece, Rome, and Byzantium.'[148]

Where East and West came together in the bazaars at the end of the silk road, we built capitals that became the crucibles of European progress. Constantinople, today's Istanbul, said Edward Gibbon, 'attracted the commerce of the ancient world'.[149] Its last Latin emperor, Justinian, fought to forge a road east, and with the wealth he won, created in Istanbul one of the wonders of Western art: the spectacular Hagia Sophia.[150] When he entered his masterpiece on 27 December 537, he is said to have murmured, 'Soloman, I have surpassed thee.'[151] And when Byzantium fell, it was to the Venetians, who became

---

148 See Amira K. Bennison, *The Great Caliphs: The Golden Age of the 'Abbasid Empire* (I.B. Taurus, 2009).

149 Edward Gibbon, *The Decline and Fall of the Roman Empire*, Chapter XVII.

150 John Julian Norwich, *Byzantium*, vol. 1, p. 266.

151 Norwich, ibid., p. 204.

the 'masters of the gold of Christendom'.[152] In the streets around the small Church of San Giacomo[153] by the Rialto Bridge, its merchants haggled for control of trade in pepper, spices, Syrian cotton, grain, wine, salt – and silk. Here, modern commerce was invented along with an extraordinary new fusion of East and West symbolised by the magnificent Ducal Palace, described by John Ruskin as the 'central building of the world':

> Opposite in their character and mission, alike in
> their magnificence of energy, [Lombards, Franks,
> Arabs]… came from the north and from the south:

---

152 Under the terms of the deal struck with the crusading princes, Venice secured three-eighths of the city and free trade in the Empire – from which Genoa and Pisa were to be excluded. Norwich, ibid., vol. 2, pp. 180–81. See also F. Braudel, *Civilisation and Capitalism, 15th–18th Century: The Perspective of the World* (University of California Press, 1992).

153 Ruskin believed the church was the first in Venice, 'the nucleus of future Venice and became afterwards the mart of her merchants'. J. Ruskin, *Stones of Venice*, vol. III (Smith, Elder & Co, 1851–53) p. 296.

the glacial torrent and the lava stream: they met and contended over the wreck of the Roman Empire; and the very centre of the struggle, the point of pause for both, the dead water of the opposite eddies, charged with embayed fragments of the Roman wreck, is Venice.[154]

There are hard economic facts that should inspire our determination to knit a new story that unites East and West, a Christian–Islamic alliance. The reserves of crude oil under the Caspian Sea are nearly twice those of the entire United States. The huge Karachaganak reserve on the border of Kazakhstan is home to 42 *trillion* cubic feet of natural gas. The mines of Uzbekistan and Kyrgyzstan are second only to the Witwatersrand basin in South Africa for the size of its gold deposits. Kazakhstan boasts great stores of the 'rare earths' vital to modern technology.[155]

---

154 See Ruskin, ibid., three volumes.

155 See Frankopan, op. cit., conclusion.

But it is the fruits of East–West fusion down the ages that should excite us most, in trade, in science and in art.

Key to the story must be a self-confident idealism, about our own values – and the ideas that we have in common.

As it happens, tolerance is one of them. Of course, religion has often divided East and West. But never as much as religion divided us in the West from each other. As Diarmaid MacCulloch puts it, 'western Christianity before 1500 must rank as one of the most intolerant religions in world history: its record in comparison with medieval Islamic civilisation is embarrassingly poor'.[156] We were burning heretics for 600 years between the first poor victims in France in 1022, and the last casualties of the practice, the anti-Trinitarian radicals torched at the stake in England in 1612. Only slowly did tolerance

---

156 Diarmaid MacCulloch, *Reformation: Europe's House Divided 1490–1700* (Allen Lane, 2003), p. 676.

emerge, from the first seeds in Transylvania's pioneering Edict of Torda in 1568, which declared, 'faith is a gift from God', and the Confederation of Warsaw four years later: 'We will not for a different faith of a change of churches shed blood.'[157] By 1616, the French minister Richelieu could argue that 'the interests of a state and the interests of a religion are two entirely different things'.[158]

Yet tolerance also has a wide and deep appeal among ordinary citizens across the Middle East, best expressed by Ibn Arabi, a twelfth–thirteenth-century Sufi mystic, who said:

> Do not praise your own faith exclusively so that you disbelieve all the rest. If you do this you will miss much good. Nay, you will miss the whole truth of the matter. God, the omniscient and the omnipresent, cannot be confined to any one creed,

---

157 MacCulloch, ibid., p. 677.

158 MacCulloch, ibid., p. 499.

for he says in the Quran, wheresoever ye turn, there is the face of Allah.[159]

That should comfort us – but it should inspire too tough conversations with our allies, whether Saudi Arabia, Qatar or Turkey, who might seek to export an intolerant Wahhabism, or arms or funds to weaponise intolerant Islamist groups fighting in Syria, such as the 'army of conquest', Jaish al-Fatah.

We should not flinch from talking about democracy. Perhaps not the Westminster model we think so perfect, but the principle. It is a good guarantee of freedom of conscience. Even the most thoughtful Islamists know that their failure to embrace some kind of democracy capable of resolving basic conflict has led to uncontrollable violence in Algeria and Egypt, ineffectual violence in Palestine, the seizure of power by the Taliban in Afghanistan, religious civil war in Pakistan, corrupt dictators in Malaysia and

---

159 I thank Dr Karen Armstrong for the reference.

Indonesia, the inability to work within coalition in Turkey and Jordan, and the bankruptcy of the Iranian regime.[160] 'If the Islamists do not succeed in resolving this problem,' wrote one leading Islamist thinker, 'they will deal a mortal blow to our hopes of Islamic renewal, and bring down calamity upon Islam. And that calamity will be far worse than any visited upon it by communism or secularism.'

Self-confident idealism abroad requires sticking true to old principles at home, such as compassion and free speech, ideas that somehow have not made it to the 'official' list of British values. Free speech has been at the core of the British miracle since the fall of the Licensing Act in 1695. In the years that followed, newspapers spread, coffee houses boomed, theatre diversified and scientific societies like the Royal Society multiplied. It was this atmosphere of diffusion – an Age of Reflection – that

---

160 The argument was well set out by Abdel Wahab al-Effendi on 29 December 1999 in the wake of Turabi's eviction from Sudan. See Kepel, op. cit., p. 362.

helped power the Industrial Revolution. Today, we already have some of the most effective laws in the world against speech that inspires or glorifies violence. We might not like the views of leaders of either the Muslim Brotherhood or Hizb ut-Tahrir, but how confident do we appear in the superiority of our values, that we have to *ban* talk of ideas we think inferior?

Surely a better approach is a conversation that celebrates the shared ideals we each have for the future, and the things we have in common in each of our communities? Too often, 'extremism' dominates the conversation that governments have with Muslim communities. What about a conversation about the good stuff? The hopeful stuff? The job of building a future? Or a celebration of the way faith – all faith – makes our country a stronger, more compassionate place, where people of different faiths make an immense contribution to building a *great* Britain. And what about working much harder together to bang this story through the media and online?

We should be practical; we know we have to inspire what some call the 'sceptical middle ground' – the 'security-worried middle-England' – but we should insist that 'we can sort out our problems together'. It must be done in a spirit of collaboration – not confrontation. There can't be taboo subjects, but we can stress a simple truth: 'No matter their faith, people in Britain don't like extremists.' None of us wants to let anyone smash what is good, not least the creation of a country where we have made huge steps to open opportunities to all – but where, of course, there is still more to do. We should be optimistic about this: England is a more tolerant and confident multicultural society than it was, even five years ago.[161]

* * *

---

161 Almost a third of people are 'very positive' about multicultural life – compared to just 24 per cent in 2011. See http://www. fearandhope.org.uk

The great biblical cities of Jerusalem and Bethlehem are only three miles apart. In the green valleys, the cream stones of the hillsides glow pink in the magical evening sunshine. But it won't be long before giant new concrete walls around new illegal settlements divide the land that Joseph and Mary crossed two thousand years ago, slicing up the border lands along the old Green Line, cutting off the villages of western Bethlehem. Yet even here, in a place where hope is running thin, someone has scrawled on the rock-face some wisdom as old as time: 'All walls fall.' East and West share Abrahamic prophets, Greek philosophy, Arabic science and millennia of history. Despite the best efforts of extremists today, walls are falling. It's the task of our generation to finish the job.